SISKIYOU COUNTY FREE LIBRARY

3 2871 00036958 3

D0952630

910.92   cop.1
Rosten, Leo Calvin
  The 3:10 to anywhere.
                                        $6.95

OFFICIALLY
DISCARDED

THE 3:10 TO ANYWHERE

Other Books by Leo Rosten

THE LOOK BOOK (ed.)

A NEW GUIDE AND ALMANAC TO THE
RELIGIONS OF AMERICA (ed.)

DEAR "HERM"

LEO ROSTEN'S TREASURY OF
JEWISH QUOTATIONS

ROME WASN'T BURNED IN A DAY:
THE MISCHIEF OF LANGUAGE

PEOPLE I HAVE LOVED, KNOWN OR ADMIRED

A TRUMPET FOR REASON

THE JOYS OF YIDDISH

A MOST PRIVATE INTRIGUE

THE MANY WORLDS OF LEO ROSTEN

CAPTAIN NEWMAN, M.D.

RELIGIONS IN AMERICA (ed.)

THE STORY BEHIND THE PAINTING

THE RETURN OF H*Y*M*A*N K*A*P*L*A*N

A GUIDE TO THE RELIGIONS OF AMERICA (ed.)

THE DARK CORNER

112 GRIPES ABOUT THE FRENCH (War Department)

HOLLYWOOD: THE MOVIE COLONY,
THE MOVIE MAKERS

DATELINE: EUROPE

THE STRANGEST PLACES

THE WASHINGTON CORRESPONDENTS

THE EDUCATION OF H*Y*M*A*N K*A*P*L*A*N

910.92
cop. 1

Calvin

LEO ROSTEN
THE 3:10
TO ANYWHERE

McGraw-Hill Book Company

**New York   St. Louis   San Francisco   Sydney
Düsseldorf   Mexico   Panama   London   Toronto**

SISKIYOU COUNTY PUBLIC LIBRARY
719 FOURTH STREET
YREKA, CALIFORNIA 96097

Book design by Marcy J. Katz.

Copyright © 1976 by Leo Rosten.

All rights reserved. Printed in the United States of America. No part of this publication may be reproduced, stored in a retrieval system, or transmitted, in any form or by any means, electronic, mechanical, photocopying, recording, or otherwise, without the prior written permission of the publisher.

123456789BPBP798765

Library of Congress Cataloging in Publication Data

Rosten, Leo Calvin, date
   The 3:10 to anywhere.

       1. Voyages and travels—1951-   2. Rosten,
Leo Calvin, date   I.   Title.
G464.R65   910'.92'4 [B]   75-26771
ISBN 0-07-053982-0

To
the memory of
MARK TWAIN
no innocent abroad

"Bring me the bow of burning gold!
Bring me my arrows of desire!"

William Blake, *Milton*

CONTENTS

□   □

OVERTURE

Whenever I yearn to see Venice again, or Taos or Hong Kong or Ottery Saint Mary, I take a token trip—in that wrinkled, grayish vehicle that weighs around three pounds and is called the brain. How easily I imagine myself back to London or Istanbul or the Valley of the Butterflies on Rhodes, to Kyoto or Portofino or Devon, sailing the Aegean toward Santorini or winding down Arizona's uncelebrated Canyons of the Walls of Gold . . .

Memory is more miraculous than magic; invisible wings waft me off on instant journeys—to Jerusalem or Jamaica or Japan. Memory, when all is said and done and endured, is the only thing any of us can truly own.

This book is not (perish the thought!) a guidebook. It is not a record of my travels. It is not a catalogue of tourist sights or sites. It is an adventure in remembrance—odd, random recollections about the unforgettable places I have seen and the astonishing people I have encountered.

Hokusai called himself "an old man mad with drawing." I may fairly be called a man with a passion for travel. My wife, who appears in many of the episodes which follow, once described me in despair: "He'll take the 3:10 to anywhere."

Ever since I was a boy, dazzled by Riverview Park (Chicago's Coney Island), I sensed what Hazlitt meant when he said, "The soul of a journey is freedom—to think, feel, do just as one pleases." The prophet Daniel said that through travel "knowledge shall be increased." But it was much more than knowledge I sought, as you will see.

So, this offbeat mixture is my personal treasury of true stories, farcical incidents, exotic scenes, sentimental ruminations, tidbits of history—and a gallery of characters unmatched in my most ingenious dreams. I hope you will find in these pages that abundance of surprise and comedy which life, anywhere I've been on this spinning globe, showered upon my innocence.

—Leo Rosten

MY FIRST TRIP: The Magic Island

I was only three when we left Lodz, where I was born, and we crossed the Polish border at Czesto-chowa. My mother's hand clutched mine, and we shivered in the cold night train to Berlin, where we were "deloused," even though my mother and I were much cleaner than the scary, smelly German guards; and she somehow found the train to Hamburg (she was only twenty-two), from which we sailed. The ship, my mother tells me, was a vile old tub called the S. S. *Rundholm,* and ours was the last trip that decrepit vessel ever made.

Ten or twelve people were crammed into our suffocating cabin below deck, and most of them were seasick, for the Atlantic was very rough that November. I wandered about the ship, looked after by strangers, my mother too sick to move from her bunk for twelve days, and I vaguely feared she might die. On the fourteenth day, everyone on the *Rundholm* jammed the rails: I saw people cry and heard them cheer, and I was held up high within the throng to see the gleam-ing goddess Statue of Liberty. We did not know it was Thanksgiving eve, nor did we know what Thanksgiving Day meant.

On Ellis Island, we were prodded and thumped and examined by doctors—especially for eye dis-eases or lung ailments; and some people wept when told they could not be admitted to the Prom-ised Land and would have to sail back to Europe. One man had three times crossed the Atlantic—

and three times been sent back to Odessa, 7,000 miles away. A sad fourteen-year-old boy had already spent eight days on Ellis Island, my mother told me, waiting to be called for, vouched for, by some relative, and he wondered if anyone would ever come, and if he ever would be wanted.

We ate at long, bare tables, sitting on benches, and we slept on iron cots in large, caged rooms, and we waited day after day, five endless days, to hear our name called. In later years, I learned that the "entrance" money my father had saved and sent from Chicago (he had left Poland for America eighteen months before) to a friend in New York had gone astray in the mails.

The wire-screened waiting chambers were packed, and each day more "greenhorns" arrived, to replace those who had been admitted and join those who still waited: wrinkled women in babushkas and mail-order brides in tasseled hats, clinging to bedsheets or bundles in which they had packed pillows and feather quilts and precious mementos of homes they would never see again; Greeks in funny skirts and leggings, forever fingering their beads; Swedes with celluloid collars; stolid Dutchmen; Turks with fierce mustaches; Russians in Cossack boots; Romany gypsies with blazing eyes, who gave me candy; and Jews with thick beards and unshorn ear ringlets, wearing yarmulkas or broad, flat hats and long, black caftans. Three times a day the Jews wound phylacteries on their left arm and placed the small, square boxlets on their foreheads, then donned white prayer shawls and faced east to worship the Lord, rocking back and forth as they sang out, then whispered, passages from their oft-kissed, well-worn prayer books.

Around me, people lay on their cots moaning, frightened and frightening, forlorn, exhausted by the voyage, undernourished, fed by kind American hands. And everywhere were squalling babes in arms, raucous children running about, and older boys and girls who tried to calm them down. The adults talked daylong of the golden land, and though I only understood Yiddish, I knew that all the motley swarm mourned the mothers and fathers, wives, brothers and sisters they had left behind, after fervent vows to work and save and send them ship's passage to America soon.

Each night we looked through the wire window nettings to Castle Garden, on Manhattan, its name twinkling in an arch of pretty light bulbs, inviting as a carnival in some nearby-yet-forbidden realm.

And when at last our name was bellowed, my mother cried with joy and seized our satchels and led me onto the ferry to Castle Garden—to New York!—and I knew that the miracle had come to pass. . . .

The train to Chicago took twenty-nine hours and was hot, and the engine's smoke and soot choked us. We sat and slept on hard caned seats; whenever I spied a Pullman porter I was transfixed, for I had never seen a black face before.

In the tumult of a cavernous Chicago terminal called La Salle, my father was waiting for us. He was waiting at the very steps we descended. But I fought to escape his wild embracing arms, crying out to my mother in my confusion. She was laughing, *"Tatishee! Tatishee!"* ("Father! Father!"), but I did not recognize him at all. For he had shaved off his dear, remembered Vandyke and was half-American now.

NEW YORK:
Forever Carnival

No city on earth demands so much, extracts so much, promises and punishes and rewards you so. Only a special breed of mortal can choose to live in New York—this triumphant island, so dazzling, so audacious, so vulgar—Babylon wed to Bedlam on the Hudson. And only a peculiar brand can love Manhattan on a hot summer's night.

Heat waves do peculiar things to people: they stun the English (a London headline: 76° AGAIN! NO RELIEF IN SIGHT); they insult the French; they inflame the Irish; they send Italians up new heights of gossip and venery. But a heat wave pushes New Yorkers inside themselves, and it is in reverie that Manhattan finds refuge from whatever it can neither master nor mitigate.

During a scorcher, New Yorkers turn into sleepwalkers, stumbling around, muttering to themselves. A honky-tonk air saturates this unreal island. The brownstone stoops sprout folding chairs, where fat women in potato-sack dresses sit with their legs far apart, and old men wear handkerchiefs knotted four-square on their heads. On bright street corners, phantoms guzzle soft drinks out of beaded bottles. Shopkeepers stand in doorways, wiping their necks and chewing stale cigars. Only the nubile girls bounce along the sidewalks, their gossamer frocks clinging to foam-rubber thighs. In the very old, rich side streets, the tar oozes between the cobble-blocks. I think that New York's sun drives tar crazy; it certainly confuses it with a promise of resurrection.

On torrid nights, the metropolis is muted in murmurings. Limp bodies festoon the fire escapes; ghosts amble across rooftops; and everywhere the air conditioners of the lucky hum like an armada of succoring bees.

In Times Square, sailors, in heat that has nothing to do with the temperature, puzzle along under the blinking marquees, or study the pictures of "50 Glamorous Hostesses!" plastered around the entrances ("Up one short flight of stairs") to temples of taxi-dance romance. At the Plaza, elegant maidens lift their gowns to wade in Diana's fountain. In Central Park, bands play Strauss and Sousa, and everywhere the grass is massed with bodies and blankets. In the carriages that clip-clop through the sylvan glades, wide-eyed tourists gape, and golden-wedding celebrants nuzzle in the spell of this astounding city on a steamy summer night.

But don't let my romanticism gull you. Quite wild, crazy things erupt in Manhattan during a heat wave, too. Here—from the maze and daze of memory—are a few.

On the shimmering desert of Park Avenue, I waited for the traffic light to change. A taxi crawled to a stop before me. The sole passenger was a French poodle, neatly trimmed and beautifully beribboned, sitting upright on the back

seat, front paws crossed, supremely composed—
who bared his teeth and (I swear) sneered at me.

I gawked at the sweating driver.

He flung a hairy arm out in disgust. "It's too
goddamn hot for the fancy dame who owns the
pooch to take him for a clip and shampoo herself.
Natch!"

✡✡✡

A walk-up flat in a brownstone on Sixty-third
Street. I was dining with the girl I would soon
marry. Suddenly, we heard a strange, soft but
heavy shuffling-plopping.

"Listen."

The peculiar swooshing came from below: ka-
lump, *whoosh*, kalump-*coosh*.

My girl said, "That man walks like an elephant!"

"You are nuts," I fondly smiled.

Klump-*shoosh*, bloomp-*whoosh*.

"What do you think it *is?*" asked my betrothed.

"Martians. They're playing leapfrog over bounc-
ing bales of kapok."

She winced, delicate even in disgust.

Pshoop-*palump*, bloomp-*shoosh*.

"Leave us end the torture of doubt, dear one."

"Gladly," dear one agreed.

We stepped to the window.

My love was right. Well, sort of. It was not a
man plopping and swooshing below us like an
elephant. It was a real elephant, in fact a long,

moody line of them, marching, trunks tied to tails, heads bobbing, ears flapping, a hundred massive foot-pads shuffling swooshily on the street.

The jumbos were on their way to work. The circus opened next morning.

From the august *New York Times:*

> Recently, a Queens salesman began wondering if he shouldn't consult a psychiatrist. Every time he drove his car, he thought it was raining. He clearly heard the sound of gurgling water, but no rain was falling.

My psychiatric consultant, to whom I promptly telephoned these glad tidings, chuckled as he offered an instant diagnosis: (1) The salesman *hated* to go out on the road; so (2) the rain he imagined he was hearing was no more than wish fulfillment; hence (3) this was a perfectly understandable expression of "the salesman's unconscious"—which, preferring to stay in bed with the salesman, cunningly produced the illusory sounds of rain in order to (4) trick the salesman into going back home at once to hit the sack.

I thanked the merry psychiatrist and hung up. I just did not have the heart to read him the remainder of the story:

> One day, the salesman headed for the nearest service station.
>
> It seems that the car's steering column was

full of water, which had accumulated from both condensation and leakage.

The mechanic told the salesman it was the first time he had ever run into such a problem.

✢✢✢

I once visited Manhattan and stayed with my uncle, who had survived four years on Devil's Island. On my first night in the luminous city, he took me to dinner in what he called his "most favorite" restaurant: "It's a place you'll never forget," he chortled. He was right.

The moment we entered, a waiter smote himself on the forehead, gazed toward heaven bitterly, and wailed, "He's back!"

UNCLE
"Back?" A man who eats here once hasn't the *strength* to go anyplace else.

WAITER
Ten thousand waiters, at *least,* slave away in New York. Why does God have to pick on me by sending you? . . . I am an atheist!

UNCLE
In this restaurant, they give you ulcers *before* you eat. . . . (to waiter) Would I hurt your feelings if I asked for a menu?

WAITER
What choice do I have?
          (offers menu)

UNCLE
(to waiter)
For the sake of my nephew here—a fine boy, a
student with a future, with a right to live—tell me
honestly: How is the chopped liver?

WAITER
The chopped liver is no worse than the pickled
herring.

UNCLE
I don't like pickled herring.

WAITER
Let me be the first to congratulate you.

UNCLE
Is the gefüllte fish, through some oversight on the
part of the management, fresh?

WAITER
To my *enemies,* I wouldn't recommend it.

UNCLE
(to me)
That means that to his *friends,* it's delicious. . . .
Two gefüllte fish. And, assuming we survive, do
you recommend the pea, vegetable, or chicken
soup?

WAITER
Mister, are you ordering a meal or voting in an
election?

UNCLE
I'm hoping, fool that I am, to get a *hint* about the food.

WAITER
For that, ask a chemist; I'm only a waiter.

UNCLE
You hide it beautifully. . . . Let me ask you, man to man: If you were in my place, what would you order?

WAITER
If I was in your place, I'd kill myself.

UNCLE
That I'll do on my way *out*. . . . I'll have the pea soup.

WAITER
Take the barley; it's better. . . . Mr. Nephew, what do you want?

I
The vegetable soup, please.

WAITER
Don't be a fool; take the chicken.
> (He brought us our gefüllte fish, then the pea soup for my uncle and the chicken soup for me.)

UNCLE
(to waiter)
That chicken soup smells de*lic*ious. Why didn't you recommend it to me?

WAITER
You didn't ask for the vegetable.

Nothing in New York is as unique as its waiters. In no city I ever visited, save Tel Aviv (where the *meltsars* act like prophets condemned to wait upon Philistines), are waiters as independent, thin-skinned, abrasive, cynical, or sardonic as they are in Manhattan. Quick to take umbrage, they reek the *noblesse oblige* of dauphins forced to serve peasants.

After prolonged digestive research (and humiliation) I have come to the following unkind conclusions:

1. A New York waiter hates to tell anyone the time. Once, eating in an abattoir near Seventy-second Street, I asked a passing menial, "Can you please tell me what time it is?"

He answered, "You're not my table."

2. When taking your order, the New York waiter grunts or growls; this makes it impossible for you to know whether he really understood you—which is part of the pledge he took during initiation into the Society for the Dissemination of Frustration.

3. He hands you the menu upside down. This is done in order to exercise the customer's wrist, thus toning up your muscles for tipping.

4. He asks you exactly how you like your meat done, so he can tell the misanthropes in the kitchen how long to overcook it.

5. He writes your order down in a secret code that is changed each morning, to prevent customers from breaking it. In this way, he can give you the wrong check, which is always larger than it ought to be. You would think that *once,* at least, a wrong check would be smaller than your rightful one; but this never happens. Economists call this the Law of Irreversible Gain; customers call it the Culinary Con.

I was lunching with my daughter in a restaurant on upper Broadway. As she was describing a hockey game with the animation of a twelve-year-old, our waiter trudged over to us on fallen arches, carrying two large bowls of borscht. He started to put one bowl down, but my daughter's hands were flying around, so he pulled back in disgust and came in at another angle of his professional hypotenuse. But now, my daughter was outlining what might have been a pregnant whale. The waiter pulled back again, drew himself up to his full 5 feet 4 inches and in steely scorn declaimed, "Lady, *make your move!*"

"I beg your pardon?"

"You expect maybe a nice borscht bath?"

"Oh, I'm sorry," said my flustered child.

"Daunt be sorry; be *still!*" He set the bowls before us with hauteur.

"Thank you very much," I said.

"So you valcome very much," said the waiter.

Where but in New York is borscht glorified by such dialogue?

One night, strolling down old Sixth Avenue, I saw a straw hat glistening in the gutter—and a woman, wearing the hat, in the same locale. I bent down. She was neatly dressed but reeked of strong waters. "Are you all right?" I asked.

"I am *not* Miss Albright!"

"Do you live near here?"

"In *these* surroundings?" she sneered.

"I'll get you a taxi."

"Sure, Sir Gladahad—get me a (hiccup) cab."

I stepped into the street and, by masterful signaling, succeeded in getting a dozen taxis to speed past me. The moment a driver spied the recumbent dowager at my feet, he gunned away, trailing uncomplimentary opinions. Though quite erect, I was called a creep; sober as a cleric, I was denounced as a lush; anxious to go elsewhere, I was told to get lost; hearty and well-tanned, I was instructed to drop dead.

A grizzled cherub finally came to a halt. "Okay, Mac," he sighed, "pour her in. In this cockamamy town, I guess you gotta help your fellowman—animal, vegetable or human, right?"

"Right." I got my hands under the boozy lady's arms. "Here we go, madame. Ups-a-daisy."

"Daisy?" she sang. "Where *are* you, Daisy?"

I plopped her through the door. "Where shall I tell the driver to go?"

"How d'*I* know where you want to go?"

"Not me," I said. *"You."*

"Damn right I'm not you!"

"What—is—your—ad-dress?" I asked.

"I (hiccup) bought it in Macy's."

"Listen. Do—you—know—where you live?"

"Shertainly I know where I live, goddamn it! I *live* there, don' I?" And thus she passed out, lost in beautiful thoughts I would never share.

As I closed the cab door, the driver nodded sagely, "So you ain't goin' with her, huh? Some pal!"

"I don't even *know* her!" I protested. "I just saw her lying there."

His smile was more withering than contempt. "You're from out of town, huh?" And away he drove.

I don't know where he took her. I assume there is a secret warehouse, somewhere in this infinitely resourceful city, where you deliver the drunk and the incoherent. Civil servants put them into holding bins, I suppose, or file them in drawers marked "Temporary."

✤✤✤

Once I stumbled out of the inferno of the subway, into Grand Central's cathedral. Around me bobbed the bleary faces of hell's damned—commuters—and a redcap, his face glistening like oiled cobalt. I heard my voice from a distance, gasping: "I . . . feel . . . ill. . . ."

"Huh?" he glared. *"What's* that?"

"I . . . want . . . lie down."

"Here?" he cried. "Man, you crazy?" The harsh chimera floated off.

Uniform looms: Brakeman? Fireman? Conductor? Male Rockette?

"Please . . . a nurse . . ." I moaned.

"You employed by the railroad?"

"I . . . feel faint . . ."

"You *can't* faint here! You're in Grand Central!"

So I was, smack in the middle of that great, vaulted expanse. "First aid?" I bleated.

"Upstairs—if you work for New York Central."

"I'll . . . take . . . any . . . job," I yammered.

"Second floor—around that pillar."

Elevator. 2. Out. Stagger. The lettering on a glass door read: NEW YORK CENTRAL/MEDICAL DEPT. In floated I. A waiting room, empty. An open door beyond. A man in overalls, groaning, bloody hand in midair. A phantom in white was bandaging it.

I saw a bench and fainted with ease. Perhaps I drowned. I may have died, for all I know. Somewhere a radio played my request number: *Götterdämmerung.* Sometimes footsteps splashed by, entering or exiting my accidental haven. But no one spoke to me. No one questioned me, no one harmed me, no one helped me. No, siree. I was in some goddamn glass cage, hermetically sealed off from doctors, coppers, robbers and New Yorkers lost in their endemic rites of indifference.

About two weeks later, a nurse leaned over me.

She was the most beautiful woman in the world. I fell in love with her.

She studied my clothes. "Hey, *you're* not a Central man!"

"No," I mourned. "I'm a remote relative."

"Oh, boy. You're a card." She called to the inner room. "I'm leaving now, Doctor."

"Where you *going?*" I whimpered.

"Weehawken." She vanished.

Later, *he* loomed over me. Charon. Mortician eyes. "You probably sweated all the salt out of your system. Stupid. Take tablets. Just close the door when you leave."

I had my revenge, by God. *I left that door open!*

That happened years ago, but it is just as fuzzy as if it happened yesterday. And every so often now, when the heat molecules jump up and down in my brain, I think I am a bona fide Central employee in overalls, stretched out on that glorious bench, munching salt tablets and sipping soda pop, in blissful suspension from the human race.

How can I end these vignettes of the most exciting, exasperating metropolis on earth? When memory, no less than inspiration, failed me, I left my desk and wandered through the steaming city.

I dawdled, oblivious of direction, my gaze drifting across faces out of Doré or Daumier, stunned by the boom and buzz of hell's traffic.

On Fifty-sixth Street, I beheld a proud placard,

tacked to the boardings around an immense exca-
vation, from whose shards and mud and ghastly
moats a fleet of dump trucks crawled up and
down, loaded with dynamited rubble:

DANGER!
COMPLIMENTS OF
VITIELLO BLASTING MAT CO.

Moments later, on Third Avenue, I passed a
roofing truck (parked, of course, in a "No Parking" zone). The name on the side of the vehicle
was "Fiedler's," and a triangular sign perched on
the truck-top read:

FIEDLER ON THE ROOF.

I fled into the relative pasture of Lexington
Avenue. A loving couple approached me, talking a
blue streak, exchanging intimacies in that un-
abashed nonprivacy with which New Yorkers
kindly enrich the lives of all within earshot.

The young man was wearing a Hawaiian shirt,
its tails drooping over his trousers—a gorgeous,
vulgar shirt on which efflorescent paint celebrated a hula-hula girl wriggling under the palms
of Waikiki. The girl wore a peekaboo blouse and a
miniskirt, with brains to match.

The lovers stopped before a surgical appliance

store, from whose windows plastic legs and elastic trusses offered comfort to the maimed, and embraced.

"Okay?"

"*Fab!*"

"You're the *most,* doll-face."

"Mmh!" She smacked a smooching kiss on his cheek.

And as the love-drenched couple parted, to attend to separate brief errands, they shouted these lyrical adieus:

MINISKIRT
So you won't be long, honey?

HAWAIIAN SHIRT
Naw, faw-fiminutes.

MINISKIRT
So okay. Hurry. The door will be open.

HAWAIIAN SHIRT
Seeya in a jiff.

MINISKIRT
(yelling after him)
And don' figgit my aphr'disiac!

I could end right here; but that would be a disservice to truth, because Miniskirt's next words, pealed towards the hula-hula dancer under the palms, were: "The *cologne*, Jack! Not the poi-fume!"

New York. Do such things happen in any other city on this whirling star?

I, THE COUNT OF MONTE CRISTO

The most famous umbrella and walking-stick shop in the world is in Piccadilly. I have drooled into its fascinating windows a dozen times, admiring the sumptuous gold—or silver—or ivory-handled canes (the English call them "sticks"; a cane is what one used to beat serfs with), the marvelous "shooting sticks" (the handle splits down to form a seat, when you weary of bagging grouse and seek rest on a moor), the splendid array of tightly furled umbrellas, as proud and meticulous as a line of the Queen's Own.

Came one day of glory, when I mustered up enough courage to enter this imposing emporium. I stopped before a special case. One of the "clarks" approached me, smiling, remarked that each "stick" contained a sword, and asked whether he could *possibly* demonstrate one. In a fit of insanity, which customarily sheathes my embarrassment, I exclaimed, *"Sword* sticks? They fascinate me!"

"And why not, sir? Remarkable craftsmanship. . . . And for what purpose, if I might ask, sir, do you wish to acquire one?"

I could hardly tell him that ever since I read Dumas and Sabatini, at fourteen, I had been possessed by a passion to own a sword. What I heard myself blurt, instead, was: "Dogs! I . . . often weekend in Connecticut, and wander about, down back roads or lanes . . ." (I *never* wander down back roads or lanes in Connecticut.) ". . .

and sometimes . . . well, one is confronted by a ferocious dog. . . ."

"Human or canine, sir?"

My expression must have reflected my awe, because the clerk added, "Doesn't matter, sir. *This* little beauty will manage either." He lifted a stout, cherry-wood stick out of the case, drew erect, then, humming to himself as if he were strolling down a deserted lane, instructed me as follows: "Well, sir, suppose one is taking a breath of air on a fine night in the country. The lane is deserted, the hedges high, the evening dark. . . . Suddenly . . . up leaps a ruffian! A ruffian . . . drunk, perhaps, from the local pub. Lurking there in wait, don't you know? He leaps forth. So . . ." My preceptor lunged the swordstick straight at me, within an inch of my breast.

He waited. So did I.

"Proceed, sir!" he frowned.

"What?"

"Act the *ruffian*, sir! Act . . . the . . . *ruffian!* Oh *do* grab the stick!" he snapped. "That would be the natural thing to do, would it not, were you the ruffian who had just *leaped* forth from a hedge to cosh a gentleman on a lonely country lane??"

"Of course." I grabbed the stick.

"*Aha!*" he cried, pulled back on the handle— and, as I clung to the stick, exposed a gleaming, yard-long blade of steel. *"Voilà!* The peril is reversed! For *I* now can thrust the blade into the ruffian's side, or arm, or *whack* him upon the head without drawing blood. In any case (you may be *quite* shaw) our reckless ruffian will be so *pet*rified by the sight of this steel that he will flee for his life!"

I gulped. He briskly removed the cherry-wood scabbard from my frozen hands, inserted the sword, handed the bucolic weapon over to me, handle forward—then lowered himself into a skulk. "Now, sir, you act the gentleman and *I* shall be the lout. My cap is filthy, my eyes are bloodshot, my manner ominous . . . I leap at you. Oh, act the *gentleman*, sir! Ex*tend* your stick!"

I extended a trembling stick. With a Neanderthal grunt he grabbed it.

"Pull *back*, sir!" he complained.

I pulled back, which exposed the shining, silvery, murderous blade.

"See? Now you can without the slightest effort lean forward, touching or piercing my shoulder, my arm, a leg. You need not"— he confided lowering his voice —"resort to the ultimate, running me through the heart. . . ."

I bought the glorious stick. In a trance of romance and euphoria, I strode down St. James's. My head was high; my eyes flashed challenge at every passerby. Not one was man enough to test my mettle.

In our hotel room, I practiced exhilarating thrusts and parries and *coups de mains* (I per-

suaded my wife to act the ruffian, white as a pil-
lowcase though she was, and more rabbit than
ruffian).

For the next week I walked the streets of London in a transport of newfound intrepidity. I saw
myself as Scaramouche, as D'Artagnan, even as
Leo the Lion-Hearted; in any case, as the foremost
swordsman of our time, peer of Douglas Fair-
banks and Ronald Colman and Errol Flynn. I pos-
itively ached for some ruffian to leap at me—out
of a pub, say, or even a mews. . . . Then I became
the Count of Monte Cristo, yearning, eyes narrowed, to accost my four dastardly foes. (Dredge
my memory though I did, I could scour up only
the names of vile Danglars and despicable Ferdi-
nand—who, you remember, betrayed Pasha Ali in
the Greek revolution of 1823.)

It was a glorious week, a week of Dumasian
dreams and Sabatinian victories, even though not
a single ruffian (*drat* the efficiency of Scotland
Yard!) crossed my path. Nor even a slathering
dog. . . .

In New York, ten days later, the customs inspec-
tor scrutinized the form on which I had listed my
purchases. His head jerked up, then down, then
up. "One *sword*-cane?"

"Yes*sir*," I beamed. "Isn't it a beauty?" I lifted
my precious cherry-wood stick and pulled the
handle back. He caught but one glimpse of the
deadly steel before he barked: "Oh, *no!* God-

damn it! You can't bring a concealed weapon into the United States!"

My glorious cutlass, my precious falchion, my invincible rapier was confiscated. You must not bring a concealed weapon into the land of the free and the home of the brave.

I suppose I should feel grateful I was not clapped into irons and hustled into the Château d'If.

King Agamemnon's Palace

It was a long, dull drive from Corinth down the furnace of the Peloponnese before we reached Mycenae, the citadel of Agamemnon. What reader of the *Iliad* would not feel a quickening of the heart? Here once stood the palace "rich in gold" of the fabled leader of the Greeks, Homer's "king of men," the hero who for ten long years (!) laid siege to Troy—commanded great Achilles, mighty Ajax, wise Ulysses who conceived the Trojan Horse. . . .

What I beheld, after so much anticipation (and perspiration), was a desolate hillock overlooking mile upon mile of the dusty Argive plain, leading to distant, vanished Sparta. I dutifully admired the Lion's Gate, in those huge, thick walls said to have been built by the Cyclops; and we found the secret entrance to the buried cisterns that made it possible for Mycenae to survive many a siege—by enemies who could not figure out how on earth (or from earth) the fastness was getting its water.

We perused the crumbled Circle of Royal Graves, tombs shaped like beehives, outside the old walls; my guidebook told me that the largest of these mortuary chambers was the Treasury of the House of Atreus, and that Agamemnon was buried with a golden mask on his features—for the Achaeans (as Homer called the Mycenaeans) were "dear to Zeus" and their monarchs were revered as gods and buried in golden masks.

But the glowing names are misleading. What we saw and clambered over was rubble—the leveled, dreary residue of a palace destroyed nearly three thousand years ago. The entire historic site covers less ground than the boys' camp I once attended outside of Kalamazoo, Michigan. We are all dupes of expectation.

Mycenae is just not worth the journey, Homer. Unless you're an archaeologist, an historian, or an Attic buff. Was it not Plato who described Greece as "the skeleton of a body wasted by disease"?

Oh, yes, I kept reminding myself that Perseus founded Mycenae, so 'tis told, and that the masterpieces of Aeschylus (*Agamemnon, Eumenides*) deserve every echo of their immortality. I choked up on the awesome evocation of names: Clytemnestra, Agamemnon's wife, and Orestes, their son. I stirred my spirit by recalling that Agamemnon returned here, from the quixotic quest to capture Helen of Troy, with none other than Cassandra, King Priam's daughter. Clytemnestra and her paramour, the dastardly Aegisthus, murdered Agamemnon as he came out of the bath, right where I stood.

As I wiped my neck and took off my wet shirt, fluttering it in the breezeless air to dry, I forced myself to face the fact that Mycenae is only slightly less depressing than an Indian burial mound in Nebraska. At this point, my mind flooded with recollections of the story of Heinrich Schliemann . . .

That astounding eccentric was so mesmerized, as a boy, by Homer, and so convinced that the

Iliad was history and the Trojan wars not mythology, that in 1873 he financed his own expedition to excavate the very ruins amidst which I shirtless stood. Schliemann went on to Anatolia, to dig and dig at the Hill of Hissarlik, badgered by Turkish officials and fuming at Turkish diggers, until he unearthed no less than seven layers of settlements—and found Troy near the Hellespont exactly where Homer had said it was.

Few feats of scholarship, few triumphs of conviction, rival Schliemann's—whom the historians and Greek *mayvonim* of the time called a crackpot. And few characters in history equal the German fantast who, lacking formal education, mastered seventeen languages, amassed several fortunes in St. Petersburg and Berlin, and became a geomaniac: he traveled through Sweden, Italy, Egypt, Syria, Carthage, India, Java, China (where he walked the Great Wall for God-knows-how-many miles). He traversed the deserts of Arabia, ploughed through the jungles of Mexico, scaled the high fastnesses of Chile and Peru. He wrote books on China, Japan, Troy, the Peloponnese.... And in Indianapolis, Indiana, if you please, he became an American citizen—because the state's divorce laws were genial enough to permit him to slough off the wife back in Russia by whom he had sired three children.

All this, mind you, before Schliemann was forty-seven. At this point, from Indianapolis, he wrote to Archbishop Vimbos in Athens to send him photographs of authentic Greek virgins who were available for marriage. Archbishop Vimbos, who had taught Schliemann Greek in St. Petersburg, sent him a slew of pictures, and Schliemann chose one of a seventeen-year-old, Sophia Engastromenos. He sailed to Athens, paid swift respects to the girl's startled parents, and wed the girl— who became his most loving, indomitable disciple in the prolonged diggings to resurrect Troy. . . .

All this mind-boggling story possessed me as I stood broiling in Mycenae. Why? Because, as I waved my sweat-drenched shirt, I remembered one of Schliemann's more remarkable self-indulgences: from Greece and Turkey, that fastidious egomaniac regularly sent his silk shirts and lavish underwear to London. For laundering. Even his gossamer handkerchiefs came back, impeccably washed and pressed, in five weeks.

I shamelessly confess it: I prefer the saga of Schliemann to my memories of Mycenae. Please, Greek friends, do not put the curse of Hecate upon me.

TO LONDON-
WITH LOVE

Warning:

I know I shall be accused of romanticizing—for I will not discuss London's fierce inflation and England's ferocious taxes, the demolition of beautiful old buildings for ugly high-rise apartments (more like refrigerators than homes), the political disintegration of both Labor and Tories, the surprising rise of muggings, burglaries and racial tensions.

I shall not depress you with data such as the cost of a gallon of gasoline ($1.76) or a pack of cigarettes ($.94) or a third-rate hotel room ($42.00).

Yes, London's clerks are sometimes curt, these days; the post offices are staffed by irritable thin expatriates from India; servants are scarce, and porters are sour.

Yet, all in all, life in London remains more agreeable, swathed in more civility and charm, than in any city shaking with the convulsions of our time.

So these entries are a quite personal, admittedly romantic view of a city and people I have known for forty years, and dearly love.

—L.R.

The Singularity of London

Of London, Charles Lamb once wrote: "I shed tears from a fullness of joy at so much life."

I contemplate "so much life" in Tokyo or Los Angeles without a solitary trickle of joy; on the contrary, I am repelled by their vulgarity. But London. . . .

What is it about London that sets her apart from other cities? We admire Paris; we are enthralled by Venice; we are electrified by New York; but one becomes profoundly *fond* of London. No great city inspires such affection. For London has the most unexpected attribute of a metropolis: intimacy. Stately, solid, ancient with grace and grandeur, London is quaint without being cute.

The immense city is really a jumble of villages—each with its own identity. No matter where you wander, you are bound to come upon greenery: a verdant square, a tiny park, fine lawns, magnificent trees. You can walk parallel to so hideous a street as Tottenham Court Road or so strident an avenue as the Strand and find yourself amidst leafy squares and flower beds aburst with color.

London is a gallery of history alive. Look one way and it is medieval; turn another and it is Palladian; look up and you behold a ballet of church spires and domes, spiky crockets and plump chimney pots on a thousand roofs.

In Rome, the symbols of the past are skeletons on display. Paris seems to have begun in the seventeenth century. In Athens the Acropolis is an inapposite ruin on a precipice in the middle of a modern, unattractive city. But London's history and heritage are visible, woven into her daily life. In the heart of the financial district I saw this sign near a hole in the pavement: "Mithraic Temple." I looked into the hole. Far below lay a sun worshipper's mound or altar.

In London the past is contemporary.

London's Mood

What gives London its singularity is the mood in which life is lived: a blend of harmony and stimulation, a joining of the stately and the snug. What London offers is a sense of solidity, security—and ease.

Here I float on a sea of amenities. People are courteous, considerate, and (let me invite your wrath) civilized. Who can count the number of times a day you hear "May I help you? . . . How very kind. . . . How thoughtful of you. . . . Thank you *so* much. . . ." A shopkeeper hastens to tell you where you can buy what, to his deepest regret, he cannot provide—and leaves his shop to point the way, or help you with a package, or find you a taxi. A stranger will make your problem his own. A Londoner takes it as a personal compliment that you like his city and the people of which he is a part. But nothing will impel a Londoner to intrude on your privacy, or allow you to invade his.

Americans find it hard to define what it is about the ambience of London that intrigues them. I think it is serenity. The core of calmness is surprising in so bustling a hive.

Within this center of world banking and trade, shipping and insurance, London seems never ruffled. Londoners are philosophical about the agitations of the world and stay contented within their insular vision.

So London oozes equanimity. It envelops daily life with patience and with moderation. England's richest asset is wisdom, that priceless distillation of experience, a calm acceptance of the absurdities and tragedies of living.

The English don't *complain*. There seem to be no crises, no dangers, no defeats which have not been survived before. During political brouhahas that make Frenchmen furious and Italians panicky, Americans angry and Japanese hysterical, the English—sigh. They suppress anxiety; they shun hyperbole. Englishmen diminish drama with conspicuous imperturbability.

To be English means to discuss, not to argue; to be tentative, not dogmatic; never to lose your temper and rarely to raise your voice.

To Walk in London

I am always surprised by how beautiful London is. Gardening is, of course, England's chief religion; it surely claims more care and love than the churches, or even the great cathedrals. Amsterdam cannot excel London's tulips (hard though you may find this to believe), nor Italy her laburnum, nor France her lilacs. Rare is the window or yard or storefront bereft of a box crammed with flowers. The crowding would make a Japanese wince, but the English think a "proper" floral display permits not an inch of bare earth to be seen.

To walk in London. . . . For a New Yorker, it is astounding not once to skid on dog-do. Blunt signs warn dog owners:

A PERSON IN CHARGE OF A DOG WHO FOULS THE FOOTWAY IS LIABLE TO A FINE OF £50.

(That's 140 bucks!)

I rarely take a stroll that fails to reward me: gaslit mews, a splendid bowfront, a fanlight like glass lace; a colonnade by Nash or a cupola by Wren; a courtyard out of Dickens, a mansion fit for an earl. The profusion of Tudor towers and Georgian gates, Gothic corbels and Victorian conceits—the "frozen music" of architecture sings before my eyes.

And shops called "Lacemaker and Sword Cutlerer," or "Strong-In-Th'-Arm," or "Sweetery and Light Repasts". Or lanes like Capener's Close, Half Moon Street, Haunch of Venison Yard. Or this sign to motorists: "Please Park Pretty".

The Blessed Parks

The parks are magnificent: immense canopies of oak and elm, centuries old, flower beds aflame with color. No radios may be played in public, praise God, to shatter the eardrum with savage "singers" celebrating youth's assault on civility.

In a foreign city, I spend Sundays in a park. There is no better place to study the people amongst whom you are (and must always be) a stranger. New York's parks are raucous: brassy laughter and vicious arguments, strutting males and gum-chewing broads. In Paris, the parks reflect the tight, taut web within which French families are encased. (No people so despise foreigners.) In Tokyo, the parks display the rigid obeisances that make every Japanese a prisoner of unquestioned codes.

London's parks are quiet. People may sit in hordes, crammed together on benches, canvas chairs, the grass itself—but the conversations are muted. The English live within cocoons of privacy, even in public.

In the parks of Rome or Madrid or Chicago, parents fuss over their children in shrill decibels. The most surprising aspect of London's parks, to me, is that the English chastise a child by *lowering* their voices. Where an Italian mother will pour out a torrent of bravura strophes, or a Bronx father hurl a minatory barrage ("F' Chris*sake*, Cholly, come back here and stop foolin' with that dog he can bite a *hole* in your neck, you dope!"), an English mother or father murmurs "Charles..." in an even, diminished tone, and Charles trots back without a squawk. He will make a pubkeeper or barrister or bobby who, on Sundays, will lower his voice to chastise his young, too.

Sex on the Grass, Alas, and in the Hay, Hooray!

One feature of London's parks is the amorous intertwinings on the grass. Petting in public seems totally incongruous amongst a people considered "stuffy." But English respect for the rights of others extends to couplings in public. It may be in "bad taste," but lovers expect passersby to be so absorbed in preserving their own privacy that they (the pedestrians) will not notice them (the lovers).

The English can't understand why Americans make such a fuss about sex. Geoffrey (later Lord) Crowther, as brilliant and sound an intelligence as I have ever known, once asked in astonishment, "Do you *really* take Freud seriously? He is, of course, immensely imaginative, especially about dreams. But all that rubbish about sex—surely he was extrapolating his own lubricious fantasies!"

I forget how I answered, but he looked at me with compassionate incredulity.

When the Rev. Billy Graham left London after an evangelical crusade, he told a press conference how shocked he had been to see the amount of libidinal acrobatics "right out in the open, in the parks." London's newspapers responded in frosty editorials: It was rude of the Reverend to stare—and unforgivable of him to comment.

I feel duty-bound to pass on to you the remark of a veddy cultivated English woman: "Dear boy, one *does* fancy a friendly roll in the hay from time to time, don't you think?"

V. S. Pritchett comments about London: "We like our police to be quiet, our ambulances discreet, our fire-engines jolly."

To this I would add "—and our sex friendly."

Whence Came the Miniskirt?

The miniskirt was born in London—not, as hasty sociologists surmised, as rebellion by young swingers against bourgeois morality. The miniskirt was the unexpected result of a tax on women's skirts. London's stenographers and salesgirls sensibly began to buy their skirts in the "junior" departments, where there was no tax.

That the ever-proper English accepted the public exposure of thighs only means that they would not dream of allowing prudery to vitiate prudence, or let personal qualms hinder the sacred right of an individual to dress, no less than think, as he/she damn well pleases.

The generous flash of "hot pants" on Bond or Regent Street has given me a stiff, albeit grateful, neck.

What? No Fog!

I first came here to study at the London School of Economics and Political Science. The city depressed me beyond description: all gray and grimy, the buildings clothed in soot—layer upon layer of soot—from the soft coal burning in a million fireplaces. London's sky was rarely clear, and often blotted by a vile blend of smoke and ash. London's fogs were as thick and pea-soupy as their reputation.

Not now. The burning of soft coal is forbidden by law: the daylight is clear, and the famous London fog is gone. Across the sky drift endless eastbound clouds. I know at last that Constable, the grandfather of Impressionism, painted skies and light and clouds he saw and did not have to imagine.

London is all spruced up, clean and polished, every street dotted with the fresh, gleaming paint which is one of the wonders of Latex. Pink, white, red, blue doors bring a gay Caribbean note to once dreary streets and squares. And everywhere, one sees the pretty awnings of French and Italian restaurants. And supermarkets. And beauty parlors. And dry cleaners! At long last Londoners have agreed that it may not actually be un-British, decadent or American to (1) eat well, (2) bathe often, (3) heat a home, (4) clean a suit.

Who would have been reckless enough to predict so historic a transformation in the mores? In Bloomsbury, when I was trying to find "digs," I would inquire where the bathroom was. The landlady or landlord would always look startled. One matron exclaimed, "Oh, dear, you're American, so you *will* be wanting to bathe, I suppose." She thereupon escorted me across a cobblestoned courtyard to a chilly cubicle over a garage where there was a decrepit tub: "Now, you drop a shilling into the meter, should you want *warm* water. . . ."

The Precious Sun

In this climate, cheeks are ruddy, headcolds frequent, spirits braced—and everyone yearns for the sun. In fact, scarcely a weather report from April to November fails to prognosticate "sunny intervals" with resolute optimism.

A truly sunny hour in London brings mass hosannas of ecstasy ("What a fine day!") and crowds rush to every open space—benches, fences, grass, the parks—to turn their faces to the healing orb of heaven.

The English adore warmth, but they are demoralized by "insufferable" heat. One July, so help me God, I read that since thermometers in the Midlands had reached 82 degrees, railway officials feared that such prolonged heat might cause the tracks to buckle. No leg was being pulled.

The weather reporters on TV tickle me. One meteorologist, pointing to the radar map, snapped, "I was absolutely shocked to learn that snow flurries have descended on parts of Scotland!"

And once I phoned 246-8091 ("Weather") to be

told, by a voice that might have belonged to Deborah Kerr: "Scattered showers . . . rahther cloudy . . . but I *do* believe the clouds will disperse by dusk. . . ."

Trivia? No. Lovely revelations of the composed—and mischievous—English character.

Englishmen and Those Odd Creatures: Foreigners

Englishmen act on the assumption (never uttered) that to be English is to be blessed beyond earthly measure. An Englishman is genuinely sorry, I think, for people who, however admirable, were not born English.

> For in spite of all temptations
> To belong to other nations
> He re-mains an Eng-lish-man.

So said W. S. Gilbert, in *H.M.S. Pinafore*, perfectly.

The English are proud; the French are vain. Where Italians weep, Englishmen wince. Germans bark; Englishmen murmur. Spaniards sneer; Englishmen frown. And when Americans cry "Marvelous!", the English sigh "Quite."

Why is this so? Because the English are taught to place a premium on the concealment of emotions. In a crisis, John Bull does, as Winston Churchill put it, "fly into a calm." They voice a deep conviction as if it were a tentative opinion.

They are made uncomfortable by a raised voice or a trickling tear. Vehemence embarrasses them.

Now, these differences in what anthropologists call "character structure" are crucial to anyone who tries to understand values foreign to his own, or comprehend conduct which departs from his ingrained expectations.

The English think "a stiff upper lip" is a sign of courage; but Mediterranean people judge a "stiff upper lip" inappropriate (why should suffering cast doubt on courage?): eyes filled with tears and eloquent expressions of consolation give comfort to those, stricken by fate, who have been raised to expect men to be *simpático.*

After long, precious immersion in three cultures, accustomed from my crib to gales of laughter and epiphanies of disaster, I have come to the conclusion that Americans treat "neurotic" as a synonym for "nuts," that Jews consider "neurotic" a synonym for "human," that Englishmen think "neurotic" quite applicable to foreigners.

The English impress some visitors as cold, at best, and arrogant, at worst. I think most English men and women are shy. No people blush so often. Even Arabs are not so easily embarrassed.

The laconic English easily turn friendly—without assuming that this makes you friends. The British seem to have only old friends: family, classmates, comrades-at-arms, fellow denizens of their club or their "local" (pub).

Pets, Pets, God Protect Our Pets!

The national love of nature is exceeded only by the national passion for pets. Everyone in London seems to own a dog, cat, canary, bunny, parrot, budgerigar, parakeet, or—more exotic—monkey or ocelot. *The same thing!*

A men's hat shop on Jermyn Street has enshrined a stuffed cat in its window, in a glass case. Pussy wears a silk opera hat, lovingly made by the haberdashers.

One morning I read this newspaper caption:

GOLDFISH SAVED FROM DROWNING

A reporter in Amersham reported that the Royal Society for the Prevention of Cruelty to Animals had recommended that a proper award be given to one Peter Humphrey, aged fifty-five, "for saving a goldfish from drowning." How this marine miracle was accomplished can best be described in the journalist's own words:

> Mr. Humphrey discovered the goldfish gasping for air on the surface of his garden pond at Hillside Crescent, Uxbridge. He fished it out and found its mouth was jammed open by a pebble. Gently he went to work and gradually eased the pebble out. Then he put the fish back into the water where it quickly recovered.
> Tonight Mr. Peter Hume, an R.S.P.C.A. in-

spector, said: "Mr. Humphrey's prompt action undoubtedly saved the fish's life. I will be preparing a report to be put before the awards committee.

"There are not many people who know that a fish could drown if it swallows too much water. I would hate to think how many goldfish owners have stood by and let a fish drown because they did not know what was wrong."

English English

When I was a young reader in the British Museum, I beheld a notice over the washbasins—a notice prompted by the number of impoverished refugees from Europe who, apparently, bathed there.

PLEASE OBSERVE:
THESE FACILITIES ARE INTENDED
FOR CASUAL ABLUTIONS ONLY.

I am always impressed by the precision, and delighted by the felicity, with which the English use our common language. My wife, phoning Chicago from London, asked, "Is this the overseas operator?"

A pitying male voice replied, "This is *one* of them, luv."

On Savile Row, an American studied himself in the mirror and remarked, "Isn't the jacket too large?"

The proprietor cleared his throat. "If you will but permit the garment to assume its natural aplomb. . . ."

Such elegant exactitude sometimes founders, of course. In one London park this notice warned pedestrians:

ANY PERSON NOT PUTTING LITTER INTO THIS BASKET WILL BE LIABLE TO A FINE OF £5.

To this, the pluperfect H. W. Fowler railed: "Those who have no litter to put into the basket must, it seems, rush away to find some."

I was stopped by a sign I saw at a bank window on Oxford Street:

SERVICE SUSPENDED WHILST CASHIER IS ENGAGED ON ANCILLARY TILL ENTRIES.

Hot damn! In Sodom (New York) or Humbug Point (Oregon) that sign would read:

CLOSED

A letter to the *London Observer* continues to echo in my grateful memory:

> Gentlemen:
> I was impressed by your article headed "Escapees." I thought it was written by a deep thinkee. But are you trend followees or trend

settees? Should you change your name to the *Observee?* That might please the most forward-looking of your readees.

—Roy Herbert.

Amerenglish

Bernard Shaw titillated two nations when he said, "England and America are separated by a common tongue." Consider these translations from the Foreign Tongue used in London:

"Ha jew dew?" (How do you do?)

"View bean ha lawn?" (Have you been here long?)

"Strawd'nry." (Extraordinary.)

"I oh quate shaw?" (Are you quite sure?)

"Praps yaw prifuh a stat you to a pict your." (Perhaps you prefer a statue to a picture.)

"Kyaw." (Thank you.)

Subtle reefs of usage impede Englishmen and Americans when they converse in our allegedly common tongue. Americans "take a vacation"; Britons "go on holiday." English phones are "engaged" where American phones are "busy." The English ask one to "ring me" where the Americans say "call me." The English go "to hospital"; Americans mosey along to "the hospital." A London doctor of "med'sin" works in his "surgery"; an American M.D. prescribes "med-i-cine" in his "office." And when Albion's heirs refer to the "loo," Americans must be on their bilingual toes to realize that what is meant is the "john."

Intonation, inflection and the cadence of sentences convey social stratification in a way American speech cannot equal. Oxbridgians stress the opening words of a statement, starting at the higher notes and sliding down to the lower, thusly: "*Do* you think him honest?" Americans reverse the harmonics: "Do you think him *honest?*" Here are variants I cherish:

AMERICAN	ENGLISH
bore	baw
again	a gain
darling	ducky
strangers	strain jaws
Aunty ("Anty")	On-tee
cheaper	cheepah
nonsense	rubbish
privacy ("pryvacy")	prihvacy
issue ("ishoo")	iss-you

More than pronunciation can knock an American for a loop in London. The first time an English maid asked me "What time do you wish to be knocked up?" I entertained a passing inclination to inform her that American men are not capable of becoming pregnant.

The first time I asked a London waitress for "French fried potatoes," she flinched: "I *don't* think Cook knows how to prepare them."

I nodded toward the next table: "The cook has already done so."

She blinked, eyed me as if I was one of those

jokers from "the States" she had been warned against, and soon brought me my steak and "chips." If you ask for "chips" in New York you may get the plastic tokens used in poker.

When an Englishman says he feels "sick" he does not mean he feels ill; he means he may throw up. A "dummy," to Americans, is someone stupid; a "dummy" in Britain is the pacifier which soothes babies. In London, you do not ride a "subway," you ride the "tube." Further mystifications:

ENGLISH	AMERICAN
dicey	confused, uncertain
poppet	an endearing person
bubble-and-squeak	a mélange of meat and cabbage
banger	sausage
"do"	a social gathering
diddle	cheat
punch-up	a smallish fight
perks	benefits attached to a job (abbreviation of "perquisites")

A Man's Town

It is a cliché to call London "a man's town." But the city so emphatically is! Compare it to Paris, the paradise of couturières and *châpeaux,* or Rome, the Eldorado of women's shoes and chic luggage. In London you can't stroll five minutes without seeing a hundred signs of masculine pride and preoccupation: pipes, headgear, boots,

guns, swords, shirtmakers, "bespoke" tailors. . . .
Many English women still wear "frocks" that re-
semble the wallpaper in third-rate hotels, and
"sensible" shoes, and hats conceived in comic
strips. But English men wear superbly tailored
suits, fine waistcoats, ties or ascots to make a peacock swoon.

The Clubs

If nothing else, that unique English invention,
the club, makes London a man's town. I mean the
men's clubs: Boodle's, the Savile, Brooks, the
Reform, White's, the Atheneum. These quiet,
waxed-leather citadels are retreats from the
clamor of the city—and the family. Englishmen
cannot abide female voices at lunch.

No club displays its name. If you don't know the
name, you're not supposed to.

Talk is the glory of the clubs: discussions of
politics and scandals and the most recondite sub-
jects (every Englishman seems to be an expert in
some field he has made his hobby), accounts of a
recent trip to Kamchatka or Yucatan, acerbic ap-
praisals of a new biography of Babbage or the
"leader" in the *Telegraph* or *Times*. Such talk has
soothed my ears for many a memorable hour.

Each club's rules testify to its own tradition.
Some of the regulations floor me. The one place in
the Reform Club (where Phineas Fogg made his
wager to go round the world in eighty days) where
you cannot get coffee is the "Coffee Room." At

the Garrick, a visitor rubs elbows with exalted members in the crowded second-floor bar; but the guest may not eat in the splendid dining hall—he is taken downstairs to a smallish "Strangers' Room."

One of the snootiest of London's male preserves is governed by rules, of which No. 12 reads:

> Nothing in the rules or intercourse of the Club shall interfere with the rancour or asperity of party politics.

Silence is mandatory in the reading and writing rooms. When an American visitor was ushered into the "Morning Room" of the Savile, he greeted me loudly. Newspapers rustled and lowered; critical eyes rose and narrowed. Later, I asked a senior member what the club rules had to say about such a *contretemps*. He knit his brow, scoured his memory, and whispered: "In the Morning Room, greetings may be whispered—but conversation, never!"

Any Englishman of consequence belongs to at least one club. A friend of mine has lunched at his haven every weekday for the past thirty-eight years. On weekends—but what club man does not then rush to his "place in the country"?

May Ladies Chatter?

The crowning sign of the all-dominating maleness is the way in which many Englishmen talk about women: *terribly* nice creatures, *most* useful around the house; terribly *decent* lot, on the whole; *consoling* companions—when you want them; *awfully* good friends; tip-*top* for seeing to the garden, the kiddies, picnics and the waxing of tables. But the dears really *are* a bit pip-pip, eh what? Mustn't muddle their pretty little heads with *serious* matters, now, must one?

Melville R. once drove me to a tea at the lovely "cottage" of high-born friends in Sussex. The sitting room, crowded with country weekenders, overlooked a lush garden. Our host engaged me in conversation about "the bloody Common Market"—an evil trick of "the Continent" to snare England's economic bounty. When he left me to greet an arriving squire, my hostess, Lady N., made small talk about the *"ghastly"* weather her "poor, dear darlings" in the garden had endured.

"But your garden is magnificent!" I said. "Those lavender flowers—what are they?"

She not only told me the name of the lavender flowers (in English and Latin) but went on to name every bush, vine, hedge, pot, border, sprig, blossom. She held forth like a demented Jacobin at the barricades, enumerating the special fertilizers, sprays, pruning, hothouse forcings, cold-storage bulbs, mulches, lotions, potions, acids. "Male urine does *wonders* for roses, you know. I have a row of buckets by the toolshed, and invite all our men guests to pee in them. I *do* hope you will relieve your fine American bladder in one of my buckets—you can't *possibly* be seen from the house. Now that catalpa, just beyond the laburnum, will be in full glory once the poppet recovers from surgery. . . ." She gabbled away for a good forty minutes.

On our way back, Meville asked me if I had enjoyed the party. "I don't mean to pry, dear boy, but I could not help noting your extremely long conversation with our hostess. It must have been excruciating."

"Well, she did set a record for monologues . . ."

He frowned. "How odd. Why, she scarcely talks to anyone."

"Well, I asked her about one of her plants—"

"You *asked* her?" he gasped. "You mean *you* asked *her . . . a . . . question?*"

"Sure."

"Then you have nothing to complain about!" he snapped. "Good God, asking that woman a question! Next you'll be telling me you peed into one of her buckets!" He sniffed with scorn all the way back to his manor.

His gardens, I may say, were horticultural jewels. Yet all he said about them was: "*Do* admire the peonies. . . ."

Taxis

Oh, the unalloyed bliss of riding in a London taxi: high, ample-footroomed, leather-seated. Why, the doors even open wide enough to admit an erect adult who isn't an acrobat. How do the English expect to twist a hip or slip a disk, the way New York cabs make so easy? And London's hacks have clean, flat floors, unlike New York's mobile garbage cans. A London cabby is unfailingly courteous. And he turns his hack on its axis, without the slightest stress or distress.

You may find this hard to believe, but a cab with a dented fender may not pick up a fare but must proceed to the garage to have the eyesore mended. And if you find *that* hard to believe, let me depress you further by remarking on how often I have seen a cabbie, waiting in a "rank," shine up every inch of his vehicle with flannel rags or huge mittens with fleece palms. And beaming.

Eccentrics' Heaven

Santayana attributed England's superlative literature to a culture which shelters "individuality, eccentricity, heresy."

This citadel of propriety certainly has a bumper crop of crackpots, mystics, hermits, moonstruck pedants and deluded quacks. This bastion of respectability has as "kinky" a night life as Singapore. This middle-class museum of good sense, endlessly tolerant, is endlessly hospitable to the potty. dotty

Englishmen lavish a protective affection on run-of-the-mill nuts and colorful outmates of Bedlam. One morning I read in the London *Times:*

WHITEHALL TRIBUTE

Sir:

Mr. F. Sanger's delightful anecdote prompts me to recall an experience with my grandfather in the early 'twenties.

An imposing figure, with flowing moustaches and draped in a cloak, he would station himself opposite the statue of King Charles I and, with the point of his Malacca cane, order *stick* any male passer-by to doff his hat and salute the "greatest gentleman who ever lived."

Strangely, nearly all did so, albeit shamefacedly. After about half an hour, a policeman would invariably turn up and gently say, "That is enough for today, Colonel <u>Cockburn</u>," and *"Coe Bur* the old boy would move on, chuckling with glee—to repeat the exact performance at the Cenotaph.

> Yours faithfully,
> Christopher Phillpotts
> London. S.E. 1

The unshakable conviction that one should be free to do as one pleases "as long as one doesn't make a bloody nuisance of one's self" makes the individual inviolate here.

The "Agony" Columns

I always read the Personal columns in the newspapers: they offer priceless peeks into the private world of people I would scarcely notice on the street, in a bus, in a queue: lonely widows who love to tat, and widowed majors who yearn to tango; connoisseurs of ormolu or Solutrean flint; avid Alp-climbers, Nile-drifters, Cambodian altar-rubbers; adventurers looking for like-minded souls to "share expenses" on expeditions up the Amazon or down the Congo. The tantalizing catalogue contains so laconic and provocative an ad as this:

> Has any Englishman lost a small brown dog on the road leaving Zagreb?

Or these:

> RUINED CASTLE wanted in remote Wales. Ghosts not feared. Write Box 1136D. E.C. 4
>
> GENUINE gypsy ornate caravan for sale, £500. Box 0681-E. E.C. 4
>
> REDUNDANT Scriptomatic machine? Write Box 2382-C.

And where but in London could you read an advertisement for a "stout, sensible brooch?"

As to nature, grand or small, ponder this appeal to ecologists:

ON WENLOCK EDGE

Sir,

Hurrah for John Dugdale's letter. As a boy I saw Wenlock Edge in trouble—natural, not manmade, trouble. I was fifteen. It was a great, tempestuous sight. I told my English master,

S. S. Sopwith, and he read me A. E. Housman's poem.

I think I still know most of AEH by heart, and as a prisoner of war in the Far East I tried to put some of the poems from memory into Latin verse. It helped in that situation. One thing leads to another. Do let us not desecrate Wenlock Edge, please.

> Yours,
> Anthony Chenevix-Trench
> Fettes College,
> Carrington Road, Edinburgh.

Kind hearts beat for innumerable causes. Newspaper ads and the Letters columns bulge with appeals for the victims of an earthquake in Anatolia, a famine in Pakistan, mistreated donkeys anywhere; funds for orphans or veterans, paupers or seamen, and for the exquisitely named Society for Distressed Gentlefolk.

No cause is too small, no crusade too peculiar. I have never lived in a city where there are so many Societies for the Prevention of Cruelty to everything from stray hamsters to nearsighted homing pigeons.

English Humor

The secret of English humor is this: understate the important; exaggerate the trivial; and when in doubt, say "Mmm." And yet, surprisingly enough, the English love superlatives, which they toss about in inverse meaning. Mundane things are *"fright*fully" cheap or "ap*pall*ingly" dear; witticisms are *"terribly"* amusing or *"fiend*ishly" clever; even the most literate Londoner is prone to use "smashing" and *"super."* But a bloody riot is a "bit of a mess," a horrendous fracas "rather awkward"—and a silly hat "absolutely *ghastly!"*

Londoners love puns. The lofty *Times Literary Supplement* captioned its review of a novel about an excessively screwed-up girl:

I AM A CHIMERA

—and headed its analysis of a German composer:

FOLLOW THE LIEDER.

The English adore slapstick. I have spent several nights at the Palladium without a belly laugh, though the auditorium howled. I found the Crazy Gang, adored by Etonians and Cockneys alike, burlesque without wit; but the audience was in convulsions. As for TV humor, the mania for toilet gags, "drag" and vulgarity escapes my risibles.

I never can tell whether the English are as amused by names as Americans are: Mr. Algernon Fonsonby-Thrumpp or Tufton Beamish (M.P.). Villages called Burnham-on-Crouch, Upper Slaughter, or Walton-on-the-Naze. Houses dubbed Wockery Lodge, Pisglebe's Gorse, or Camilla

Lacey—they make me smile. This mystifies our English cousins.

Gems from the Post and Press

No matter how dark the political prospect, how disconcerting the follies of Parliament, I warm my heart in the grace of England's mores. One morning I received a letter from Her Majesty's Royal Post Office:

> Dear Sir/Madam:
> You recently posted an air mail letter to New York, N.Y., U.S.A. which was prepaid only *10½p.* The correct postage was *15p.*
> If we had sent the letter on, your correspondent would have had to pay a surcharge. We were sure you would not have liked that to happen, so we made up the postage to the correct amount and sent on your letter fully stamped.
> You now owe us *4½p.* I should be grateful if you would stick postage stamps for this amount in the space below and post this prepaid card back to me.
> > Yours faithfully,
> > E. A. Lovegrove,
> > Controller.

(If you ever run across a controller as happily named as E. A. Lovegrove, call me.)

When the mails fail to delight, I restore my faith

in England's unique ways by returning to the "Letters to the Editor." Consider this heated exchange on consecutive days:

BROKEN SHIRT BUTTONS

Sir: My grandmother used to complain that the laundry broke shirt buttons in half. They still do. May one ask why there has been no progress?

> Yours faithfully,
> Bryan Welch
> Downing College
> Cambridge

BROKEN SHIRT BUTTONS

Sir: Mr. Welch is surely mistaken in thinking there has been no progress since the days when his grandmother complained that the laundry broke shirt buttons in half. On the contrary, recent advances in laundry technology have made this a growth industry. Not only is there an exponential increase in the number of buttons broken, but they are now much more efficiently smashed, into at least half a dozen pieces.

> Yours, etc.
> C. A. Fisher,
> School of Oriental and
> African Studies

BROKEN SHIRT BUTTONS

Sir: I do not remember my grandmother complaining that the laundry broke shirt buttons in half. But she did complain about the trivia that appear in the *Times* correspondence columns. May one ask why there has been no progress?

Yours faithfully,
Richard Wood
44 Ingarsby Drive
Evington, Leicester

" Lester "

The seers of the *Times* did not stoop to defend their judgment.

If you ever fear that the invincible aplomb of Albion is, like its economy, "going down the drain," the parade of tidbits in the daily press will restore your faith:

Overhead in the foyer of one of our grandest hotels:
Young lady to old lady seated on a shooting stick: "But, Granny, why not sit in one of the large, soft chairs?"
Old lady: "One *never* sits on a hotel chair, my dear. One never knows who has been sitting here before."

I doubt that Noël Coward ever coined a niftier line.
Or feast your eyes on this:

In Kirby Misperton, zoo officials paid out more than £280 to visitors last year: for articles stolen from them by monkeys.
The monkeys specialize in snatching eyeglasses from the wearers' noses when visitors

bend forward to make out a sign on the cage which reads:

WARNING—THESE MONKEYS SNATCH GLASSES.

And here is a doozy:

> SUIT THIEF IS WORSTED
> London, September 24—As Bernard Hill walked along the street, he saw another man wearing his best suit. When he angrily demanded it back, the thief stripped off the suit and ran away in his underwear.

I can think of few things more discombobulating than meeting your own suit walking toward you, and few sights more rewarding than that of the heister fleeing down the street in his skivvies.

Best of all, this report in the London *Telegraph:*

> A man who removed a stuffed tiger from a zoo's publicity display at Waterloo Station got no farther with it than the taxi rank.
>
> The police arrived as he was trying to get into a taxi-cab with the stuffed animal, with the help of the driver and a porter. The tiger, a rare Sumatran specimen valued at £500, was too big to go into the vehicle.
>
> At Croyden Crown Court, Samuel William Smith, 50, was found not guilty of stealing the tiger. Smith told the court that while he was looking at the display, a youth told him he could have the tiger for £35. "He said that as the exhibition was closing that night, the stuffed animals were for sale cheaply.

"I thought it was a bargain at the price; but because he was so young, I hesitated. He suggested I phone Chessington Zoo for confirmation, and wrote down the zoo's phone number.

"I went straight to a kiosk and rang the number. A man replied: 'Zoo. Can I help you?' I said I was interested in buying the tiger in Waterloo Station and could he confirm that the price was £35? He did.

"A railway policeman came to the taxi and asked me where I was taking the tiger. I said I was taking it home to my wife. He arrested me for taking the animal without permission of the rightful owners."

Smith told the court he now believed he had been hoaxed. "The phone number the youth gave me must be that of another phone box right in Waterloo Station."

The Aristocracy

We lunched at the pretty cottage of friends, a scientist and his wife, who spend their weekends and holidays there. The cottage used to be the gatekeeper's lodge of the enormous estate which rolls up to the five-hundred-year-old castle which Lord B. inherited.

I asked the scientist about his lordly neighbor.

He shrugged. "Not our kind. . . . More pudding?"

"Have you ever been invited to the castle?"

"Heavens, no," said his wife.

"Have you ever met him?"

"Often. In the village. Pleasant enough fellow. Collects regimental insignia, I believe. He walks about his grounds for *hours* with one or another dog. There must be thirty in his kennels. Sometimes we hear them all barking like banshees. Frightful din."

"His family must be very distinguished," said my wife.

"Oh, yes," our host sighed. "The title was given to a pirate sea captain who plundered the Caribbean for Queen Elizabeth. Will you have coffee? ... There's a distinct strain of dottiness in the line. His great-grandfather was a drunkard. His father gambled like a fool—so he had to sell off parts of his land, like the piece we own. His grandmother has a score of lovers, including at least one duke and two ambassadors. His wife is charming—opens flower shows and hospitals—but her intelligence is either undernourished or genetically deficient. . . . Do you take milk with your coffee? Sugar? . . . As I said, they're not our kind."

Dial 192

My wife dialed 192. A male operator answered.

WIFE

Is this Information?

MALE VOICE

Well, madame, *we* call it "Enquiries." Never you mind. May I help you?

WIFE

I'm trying to find the number for a pub on Beau-
champ Place—

OPERATOR
(wincing)

I believe you mean "*Bee*cham" Place. Silly, isn't it,
the way we pronounce "Bochamp"? Upsets our
French visitors terribly. And what is the name of
the pub, madame?

WIFE

It's a "Mister Benson"—or "Benton"—

OPERATOR
(startled)

"*Mis*ter?" For a *pub?!*

WIFE

Yes.

OPERATOR
(stiffly)

I have never heard of it.

WIFE

Don't tell me you know the names of all the pubs
in London?!

OPERATOR

I like to think I know *most* of them, madame.
That's why I questioned the "Mister" with some
confidence. . . . Would you happen to remember
the *number* on Beecham Place?

WIFE
No. But it's only a block long—so couldn't you
just run down the addresses—

OPERATOR
Of all the pubs in London?! That would require
*consid*erable effort, madame. There are over six
thousand—

WIFE
My God!

OPERATOR
I don't think He arranged the number.

WIFE
But this is a new pub—so couldn't you just scan
New Listings?

OPERATOR
(sighing)
You shall have to be patient.
(under breath)
"Mast and Yardarm" . . . "Mews and Falcon" . . .
well, *well,* you *are* in luck, madame! It's "Mister
*Ben*tley." Fancy that, for a pub. *Quite* unusual.

WIFE
That's why I remembered it.

OPERATOR
I should have thought he would have chosen
something more traditional: "The Golden Horn"

or "Lord Nelson's Arm." By the way, have you ever been to "The Prospect of Whitby?" On the river—

WIFE
Yes. Adored it.

OPERATOR
I really should pop down there one day. . . . Would you care to jot down Bentley's number?

WIFE
My pen is practically panting over my pad.

OPERATOR
We must take it out of its misery. The number for *"Mis*ter Bentley's Pub" is—(gives number).

WIFE
I knew you would find it!

OPERATOR
I never could have done so without your moral support.

WIFE
Thank you.

OPERATOR
Not at all. We're not such a bad lot after all, are we?

WIFE
(laughing)
No. 'Bye now.

OPERATOR

Ba-bye, ducks.

Manners

An invitation to dinner reads "7:30 for 8"—
which means you may arrive at the former time
(for drinks) but dinner will be served promptly at
the latter.

During a formal meal, the waiter whispers the
name and vintage of each wine into the ear of
each guest. (A flustered American tried to tip
him.)

Politics does not much affect invitations; violent political enemies dine quite amicably at the
same table.

But (and what a "but" it is) you are introduced
to other guests in a sort of strangled discomfort,
with agonized mumbles. The English assume that
anyone of consequence knows everyone else. We
have attended large parties without being introduced to more than one or two total strangers.
Not that the formality would have been enlighten-
ing. I have never mastered my befuddlement over
gargled presentations such as "Butf *course* y'
know Tottie . . ." or "*Do* say hullo to dear
Midge!" or "Ah, here comes our *pet* Fldgnk. . . ."

Since an English man or woman rarely seems
capable of mustering up enough courage to ask
you what *your* name is, I have fallen into the same

cowardly custom. I know a dozen natives as "Poopy" or "Ian" or "Widge." Some day I'll grow bold enough to ask my host if they have last names, too.

The most frustrating part of it all is that I am often addressed as "Rosten"—but can't respond, as I'd like to: "Yes, Farthingale-Cummerbund the Third." Instead, I spend long, convivial evenings addressing others in the strophes to which they are accustomed: "My dear chap," or "Well, well, madame," or even "I *say*, sir." . . . In time, it becomes *fright*fully diverting.

The Stately Homes

Few Englishmen today regard the aristocracy with either reverence, humility or awe. They speak with mild amusement (or disdain) about those once considered nature's noblemen.

The English do enjoy royal pomp and princely circumstance, but behind the pleasure is an interior smile, a fond or derisive chuckle.

The rudest personages in England, of course, are the aristocrats: it is perhaps their last exclusive privilege. The titled nabobs are reeling under the exponential impact of punitive taxes and tremendous death levies. And Labor governments' periodic democratization of the House of Lords via new Labor lords and Life peers (journalists, trade union officials, economists, an actor), whose titles are not passed on to their progeny, has dealt dire blows to the heirs of ancient escutcheons.

Few illustrious lords can even maintain their stately homes, those stupendous palaces in the countryside, without luring tourists by the thousands through the ancestral gates, to pay for the privilege of trudging down the hallowed halls and salons. The revelation of accumulated wealth is staggering: acres of priceless paintings, mountains of silver, platoons of family portraits (by Van Dyke, Romney, Lawrence), exquisite crystal, miles of antique furniture, armor, costumes, libraries and memorabilia worth more than a king's ransom. As for the gardens and lakes, the sculpture and greenhouses, the pergolas and gazebos—the mere recollection numbs my vocabulary.

You can take a London bus to a dozen stately homes in the environs. I have been an enthusiastic "tripper" on excursions to Hatfield House, Woburn Abbey, and (savor the name) Luton Hoo.

Once my wife mentioned to an upper-class friend that we had just been through Knole, the great home of the Sackville-Wests.

"They're de*light*ful hosts, aren't they?" smiled our friend.

"Oh, we weren't their guests! We just paid our two shillings each, and went through."

Our friend reached for a restorative potion. "You mean you went through someone's home without being *invited?* Oh, dear. . . ."

Portobello Road

We used to go there on Saturdays for the bar-
gains in that raucous bazaar of antiques, gew-
gaws, and shameless junk. Now Portobello Road
is one of the tourist attractions of London.

Awninged carts jam the streets: a cornucopia of
fine china and silver and queer keepsakes, Victorian albums, copper kettles, true jewels,
bronzes, gout-stools, fireplace "dogs," useless
knickknacks to make Rube Goldberg drool, and
bric-a-brac commemorating Waterloo, Disraeli,
Nelson, Gallipoli. Churchill adorns Toby Jugs
galore.

But more startling than its hodgepodge wares
are the characters who now preen down Portobello Road, the hippies who sit in its gutters playing guitars, the "folk singers" who drivel about
their plight in a heartless, evil world.

I always thought Greenwich Village the lodestar
of exhibitionists, or San Francisco the El Dorado
of zonked-out freaks. Neither holds a candle to
the kooks of Portobello Road. Here I saw Rasputin
hug Lawrence of Arabia, and an English Eskimo
pick up a negroid Madame Pompadour. Unclean
girls and unshorn boys parade their "liber-
ation"—with Muslim fezzes, Cossack boots, Eliz-
abethan jerkins, seedy turbans. I don't suppose
you'll believe I saw Abe Lincoln in a stovepipe hat,
and orange bell-bottomed pants.

The best comment on this rave new world was

volunteered to us by a cheerful Cockney (greasy cap, muffler, dead cigarette drooping from lip), to whom I said, "It's really fantastic."

"Mate," he sighed, "it comes from an imbalance in the chromosomes."

Ta, ta.

Peculiar Pomp and Odd Circumstances

One expects Italians to put on operatic celebrations, or the Chinese to splurge on gorgeous spectacles. But stodgy Englishmen?

The fact is that this eminently proper, low-keyed people nurse a passion for pageantry and a genius for panoply. White-plumed helmets and crimson capes, exotic shakos and splendiferous uniforms explode color across London's reaches. Even the buses and postboxes and telephone booths (modeled on Wren's design) are scarlet.

Englishmen preserve the past with ardor. The following festivals are advertised in a guidebook:

'Obby 'Oss Day (at Padstow)
Gawthorpe Feast (in Ossett)
Beating the Parish Bounds (London)
Blessing of the Wells (at Bisley)
Cheese Rolling (at Coopers Hill)
Blessing the Sea (at Hastings)

My favorite is the Flitch Trials in Great Dunmow. In this ancient ritual, a "flitch of bacon" is awarded to that married couple who can persuade a court-of-the-manor that they have not had a single quarrel, nor once regretted their marriage, for the preceding year—plus one day. Why 366 should be more persuasive than 365, I cannot tell you.

Kidneys in Mayfair

The conversation of upper-class Englishmen mixes affection with a kind of ceramic rudeness. Consider this conversation I overheard in a posh restaurant between a blasé young man and his beautiful date:

YOUNG MAN

What on earth does that chap—the one who keeps sniffing around Cynthia—actually *do?*

GIRL

I *think* he's studying to be a dentist.

YOUNG MAN

A dentist? . . . Good God! Why would anyone want to spend one's life peering into strange people's mouths? . . . Still, I suppose it's no worse than staring into other orifices of the body, the way obstetricians or proctologists . . .

GIRL

Ron-nie, *please.* I'm digesting. . . . I *adore* sweet-breads, don't you?

YOUNG MAN

Ugh. I de*test* vital organs drowned in protesting butter.

GIRL

Um. . . . Will you share a treacle tart?

YOUNG MAN

Under *no* circumstances, thenk yaw.

GIRL

You're disgusting.

YOUNG MAN

Quite, dear heart. . . . Shall we pop in on Pinky and Fran?

GIRL

Oh, let's do. He's *fab*.

YOUNG MAN

She's not altogether repulsive, you know.

GIRL

She's balmy.

YOUNG MAN

Had enough to fill your pretty little tummy?

GIRL

I've *gorged*. . . . *So* good.

YOUNG MAN

Waituh! Bill, please. Afraid we simply *must* dahsh.

WAITER

Very good, suh. . . . . Shall I summon a taxi?

YOUNG MAN

That would be *most* helpful.

WAITER

A pleasure, suh.

YOUNG MAN

You're very kind.

WAITER

Thank you, suh. I trust everything was satisfactory?

YOUNG MAN

Quite. Come along, sweetie. Don't forget your
ghastly purse.

GIRL

Pig.

WAITER

Good ahfternoon, Madame . . .
(accepting tip)
Oh, thank *you,* sir.

YOUNG MAN

Nonsense. Cheerio.

GIRL

Ta-ta.

WAITER
(beaming)

Ta.

English Character

How would I characterize the English in a few words? I can't. But were you to twist my arm, I would say the quintessential word is—character. The English respect character much more than money or brains or lineage. (A London friend said of a celebrated writer: "He is indecently intelligent.")

What do I mean by. "character"? Personal probity; one's obligation to others; the assumption you can rely on the inherent decency and courage of "our chaps"; the ingrained respect for the right *if only* of men and women to lead their lives as they choose, without the authorities "mucking about" or nosy neighbors minding what is "none of their bloody business." England is the bastion of individual freedom.

The most powerful epithet in English English is "Shame! Shame!" One is surprised the first time one hears the word shouted by members of Parliament in debate, not the second.

Santayana, years ago, wrote these illuminating words:

> England (is) the home of decent happiness
> and a quiet pleasure in being one's self . . . a
> modesty in strength entirely absent from the

effusive temperament of the Latin (and) German dense vanity and officiousness. . . .

These self-effacing Englishmen, in their reserve and decision, seem to me truly men. . . . The low pressure at which their minds seem to work shows how little they are alarmed about anything: things would all be managed somehow. They were good company even when they said nothing.

The Englishman establishes a sort of satisfaction and equilibrium in his inner (self), and from that citadel of rightness easily measures . . . everything that comes within his moral horizon.

I do not delude myself into thinking that all the inhabitants of this island are do-gooders, or devotees of the Brotherhood of Man. On several train rides recently, I ventured into the W.C., to behold graffiti, scratched on the mirrors or scrawled on the walls, that made my blood run cold:

GOD DAM ALL IRISH!
KASTRATE SCOTISH KIDS!
BLACK BASTARDS—GO HOME!!
KNIFE YOUR WHITE FORMEN BEHIND
LOCO SHEDS!
NIGGERS ARE TRASH!!
***BURN* WHITE VILLAGES!**
SPIT ON HINDUS AND WOGS!

(I omit the anal and urinary flourishes.) But such racist pathology is found in a tiny minority.

I will argue, without the slightest hesitation, that all in all Britain remains the most decent and civilized country on this rancorous globe. These *oh gush!* people, an astonishing mélange of breeds old and new, have managed to harness prejudice. They are beholden to one paramount value: fairness. They venerate justice. They live within a code whose most potent prohibition is that some things simply "aren't done."

Custom, not ideology, governs "this island race." And English custom is rooted in moderation and a commitment to self-restraint. Absolutism is distrusted; dogmas are dismissed. If there is one thing about which an Englishman is certain, it is that it is unwise to be certain.

I remember a line Sir Denis Brogan once tossed off in his ebullient manner (he was as erudite as he was ebullient, even when sober): "To ask an Englishman for a definite opinion is bad manners."

Dear, dead Denis once wrote: "No nation is less subject to the panic of internal treason. . . . When disaster comes, the Englishman doesn't look for a scapegoat; he looks for a leader. He does not ever think he has been betrayed—merely that his affairs have been mismanaged."

The British masses adored Churchill in war, but thought him too doctrinaire to wield authority in peace. The English prefer "sound judgment" to bright theories. They are drawn to the reasonable, not the rational. "It is essentially English," wrote J. B. Priestley, "not to allow the intellect to decide everything: it must submit to some shaping and

colouring by the instinctive and the intuitive."
Woe to those who display brilliance instead of
"good sense."

The English don't like change. They have a propensity for letting things alone. Whatever the
trouble, they feel that in the long run "we'll jolly
well muddle through." Their talisman is stability.
Victoria's Prime Minister, Lord Melbourne, who
was gloomy about politics and opposed to innova-
tion, once said that the best thing about the
Order of the Garter is: "There's no damned
nonsense about merit in it."   *perfidious Albion ?*
                                            A sorry History

The English reputation for "perfidy" or "hypoc-
risy" stems from a predisposition to be practical.
Whitehall avoids inflexible positions and defers
painful decisions. When the English are uncertain, they delay. When threatened, they stall. But
when attacked, they fight like lions.

Coda

In the abounding amiability of London, I often
recall Samuel Johnson's fiat: "The man who is
tired of London is tired of life, sir; for there is in
London all that life can afford."

I find London, quite simply, the most engaging
city I have ever known—endless in kindness, im-
measurable in charm, lavish in the rewards it
offers any who come here with an open mind and
a receptive heart.

☐   ☐

HIGH TEA IN LENINGRAD

We were thirsting for tea, Mikhail and I, and headed for the huge restaurant in the huger Park of Culture and Rest. "Culture and Rest." (Why is the language of bureaucrats always clumsy—and funny?)

I should tell you something about Mikhail. He had attached himself to me (I was not entirely attached to him) as my guide, interpreter, and slicer of red tape. "I gat you in *any*place!" He was a fervent Communist Party Member. He flashed his Party card as if it were the Red Star. He could even board trolleys at the front, along with pregnant women.

At first I thought Mikhail spent every free hour with me because he yearned to improve his stilted English. Then I thought his zealous guardianship arose from his passion to "make propogonda" for the Cause on any and all occasions, and perhaps—God (oops: Marx) willing—even convert me to the One True Faith. During a brief siege of paranoia, I even wondered if Mikhail was a counterintelligence agent, assigned to foil my putative mission for the CIA: to flood the offices of *Pravda* with Alka-Seltzer.

All these unworthy suspicions crumbled before the evidence which daily accumulated: Mikhail's Marxist principles in no way interfered with his appreciation of fine food, vodka and caviar—for all of which I picked up the tab. Whenever a bar check or food bill was set before us, Mikhail went to the men's room. Rarely have I seen so persuasive a demonstration of Economic Determinism.

Nor did Mikhail's dedication to "Marxismus-Leninismus" conflict with his lifelong hobby: collecting money. He was especially fond of the color and design of capitalist currency. He gave me rubles for my dollars—netting a mere 15 percent for the friendly accommodation.

Now, Mikhail led the way to a table near a window. "Here is bast!" he proclaimed. Mikhail was prone to burst into definitive proclamation about anything—from Russia's production of pig iron to the cholera raging in Philadelphia. (What cholera? "Copitolist Amarican prass" had cunningly suppressed the news which, if made public, would inflame proletarian forces throughout the West.)

A waiter appeared, handed each of us a menu. He did not seem enthusiastic about handing each of us a menu, and I could not blame him once I saw, from the spots and stains, that the menu was an historic document. As I studied the Rorschach pattern, Mikhail studied the waiter. *"Tovarishch,"* he smiled, with consummate and fraudulent innocence, "you ondrostond English . . . ?"

The waiter reacted as if he had been insulted in Assyrian. *"Kak? Kak? Ya ne ponimayu!"*

"Good," Mikhail informed me. "He do not ondrostond. So we can talk. He is *bod.*"

"Why is he bad?" I asked.

"I no like this mon. Reoctionary."

I glanced at the waiter, who only looked cross-eyed.

Mikhail hissed, calling my attention to what the

waiter was doing. What was the waiter doing? He was mopping the table, yawning. "You see?" observed Mikhail severely. "Look how he worrk. Vary slow. No care. Sauvyet Union *bleed* from soch sobotage!" Mikhail could spot sabotage in a baby carriage.

The waiter finished plying his disheartened rag, placed his hands on his hips, and regarded us with disapproval.

"You see?" growled Mikhail. "Bourgeois!"

"Why is he 'bourgeois'!"

"He have no lov for worrking class."

"Perhaps he just wants us to order."

"His job is to *wait,* no ordrer!" Mikhail tapped the menu. "Bast we hov tea, bons and botter!"

"Fine."

Mikhail gave the waiter the order in gravelly Russian, adding *"Spasibo"* with the utmost sarcasm.

The waiter reclaimed the antique menus and trudged to the kitchen like a Volga boatman.

"Abot Gorky," said Mikhail, resuming the highly cultured discussion we had been having in the Park. "He *was* for poor pazent, *moujiks.* He *did* describe the tarrible honger and slafe conditions. But he did not ondrostond Marxist *t'eory!"*

"Surely he was one of Russia's most important authors . . . ?"

"Nyet! Important comms from aducating proletoriot!"

The voice of the waiter cut in. Mikhail looked up. The waiter said something. Mikhail smote the table. The waiter flinched. Mikhail fumed. The waiter slunk away.

"What's wrong?"

"He forgat!" railed Mikhail. "How you like? *Two* small order: tea, bon, botter—and he say he forgat! *'Two* tea?' he ask me. *'Two* bon? *Two* botter?' . . . This is how he make his slowdown! Rotten sobotage." Mikhail mourned his country's plight. *"Papirósa?"*

I produced cigarettes. (Whenever Mikhail used *"Papirósa?"* he was requesting, not offering.)

Mikhail exhaled a cloud of smoke. "So lat's comm back now on Gorky."

"Lenin admired him," I faltered.

"Lanyin, Lanyin! Lanyin always too *kind*. . . . Gorky was not Marxist in *heart!*" Mikhail tapped the area on his chest where Maxim Gorky was politically deficient.

"What about Tolstoy?" I asked.

"Lev Nikolaevich? Bah! Mysticer. Religious. Good heart, bot small brain for politics. *War and Peace* is good. Showed rotten Tsarist oristocrocy. *Anna Karenina?* Too romontic. Pastry."

A steaming glass of tea slid before Mikhail, and another before me. Then our waiter deposited a plate containing two buns, and another containing two slices of pumpernickel: on each piece of pumpernickel reposed a 2-inch square of butter.

Mikhail took one look at the pumpernickel and bellowed (I assume): "Why you bring pomprenikol? Who did order *pomprenickol?!"*

The waiter studied Mikhail hatefully. *"Zhd kyamya bo grodzhni kok svertnoff kak lubyiski!"* (That's how the phonemes sounded to me.)

"Chto? Kntz? Cysoki?" With this bellow, Mikhail turned to me, his cheeks purpling, "He say the pomprenickol-and-botter is *one unit!* He say brad-and-botter cannot be divorce! We did not *order* brad and we do have two *bons*—you see, bons—" he tapped the plate on which the buns rested "—but this beeg fool waiter say all botter must be on *brad,* so you must pay for brad becowse brad-and-botter *is one unit!"*

The waiter, divining Mikhail's exposition, removed the bread-and-butter. Mikhail almost tore the varlet's hand off as he snatched the plate back. The waiter poured out a torrent of Russian. Heads turned to us from every table in the vicinity.

"Tovarishchi!" roared Mikhail, addressing his fellow workers. *"Cysok ya probnyoski"* (a Russian dictionary won't help you)—denouncing the ludicrous ruling that butter could not be obtained *sans* pumpernickel.

An impassioned brouhaha ensued. Though conducted in Russian, its content was clear to me. The waiter displayed a menu which clearly showed that bread and butter were treated as one unit.

Mikhail protested that such a menu was unfair to the working class.

The waiter thundered that the menu had been debated and constructed *"in committee"*!

Mikhail howled that he would bring the committee's outrageous decision to the attention of the Commissariat for Food Consumption *and* the Central Tourist Bureau, who would realize the impression which such a lunacy as "bread-and-butter-are-one-unit" must make on illustrious visitors from abroad.

The waiter sneered that menus in the Park of Culture and Rest were not designed to kowtow to intellectual lackeys of American imperialism.

Mikhail bellowed that it was precisely this kind of unprogressive thinking that was giving the Revolution a bad name abroad.

The waiter snarled that Mikhail's opposition to an official menu verged dangerously close to Deviationism.

"Bozhe moy!" Mikhail thundered. *"Kak zhdrovni kak nudvoy!"* (I can't help if that's how it sounded.)

The waiter leered that he would be only too happy to remove the bread—

"But leave the botter!" snapped Mikhail.

"Never!" cried the waiter.

A women near us hissed *"Shnidz! Shnidz!"* ("Shame! Shame!")

Mikhail quoted Marx.

The waiter quoted Engels.

Mikhail retorted with a cutting quotation from a recent ukase of the Central Executive Committee.

The waiter flushed, flinched and faltered, fearing exposure as a Sloth Who Did Not Keep Up with the Party Literature.

"*Tovarishchi*," I intervened. "Take the butter *off* the bread, and put it on the buns. Then take the bread away. That would leave us with tea, buns and butter."

Mikhail's face lighted up. "Bravo! You are Marxist!"

"What?"

"Marxist! You put t'eory *with* proctice!" Grinning, Mikhail outlined my stratagem to the waiter in triumphant trophes.

The waiter shot me a glance of hostile admiration, and began transplanting the butter from the bread to the buns. Suddenly the waiter stopped. "*Nyet, tovarishch, nyet!*" Firmly, he plopped the patties of butter back upon the bread. To Mikhail (who repeated it to me in English), he said, "*If I* take the butter off the bread and place it on the buns, then I will have *four pieces of bread without butter!*" He turned on his heel, as final as he was logical, and stalked away, humming the Red Army March.

Mikhail buttered his bun in furious silence. The pumpernickel lay stricken: unused, mutely accusatory.

As I paid the bill, Mikhail growled and raised a clenched fist. "The sobotage. The sobotage! We must fight him on hondred frohnts!"

VENICE:
The Twilight of
Splendor

At a posh dinner for twelve in a Fifth Avenue duplex, our hostess, recently widowed, told us how much she had loved a consoling trip to Europe—except for Venice, "which I simply *loathed.*"

I voiced surprise.

"No one tells the truth about Venice," she declared. "The canals stink, the palaces are crumbling, and that cathedral of St. Mark came right off a tinseled valentine. It's all too corny for words."

"When were you there?" my wife asked.

"In August. Oh, I know people warn you about Venice in August, but I certainly shouldn't want to be there in *winter.* It must be like Coney Island, boarded up."

"In winter . . ." I stopped, flooded by the memory of the first time I saw Venice. I was twenty . . .

How can I convey the excitement with which I boarded the *vaporetto?* I had read a great deal about Venice, and been spellbound by the pictures I had seen in books and museums: by Guardi and Turner, Veronese, and—of course—Canaletto. A thousand images of splendor clamored in my mind.

The magnificence of Venezia had captivated kings and sultans and the lords of wealth from all the world. Where else was there so romantic a setting, so opulent a pleasure ground? After Philippe de Commines, the ambassador from France in the fifteenth century, beheld the Grand Canal, he wrote:

> It is the fairest street, I think, in all the world . . . lofty palaces faced with white marble from Istria, inlaid with porphyry and serpentine. Within, they have gilt ceilings, ornate chimney pieces, bedsteads of gold, their portals the same, all gloriously furnished. This is the most triumphant city I have ever seen.

The Venetians had a genius for pageantry and a passion for frivolity: *fêtes* and *soirées,* immense regattas and masquerade balls. St. Mark's Square was a constant carnival as magicians and acrobats, jugglers and jesters performed before pretty tents and booths. Life was a rondo of endless flirtations—enhanced by masks (used by men as well as women) held on silver or ivory handles. The paintings of Guardi and Longhi chronicle the elegant coquetry of public amour.

On the day dedicated to Mark, the patron saint, every Venetian husband gave his wife a red rose. Every bride was officially required to have long, long hair—into which golden threads were intertwined. Widows could be married only at midnight, veiled, and all in black.

In the grand religious processionals, white miters and scarlet cassocks accented monks' brown cowls to proclaim the glory of Christ. Apparel of astonishing beauty glowed in the light of a thousand hand-held candles. Cavaliers paraded in tricorn hats and plumes, slippers buckled in silver, harlequin breeches, cloth-of-gold doublets. The low-bodiced ladies strolled in gossamer veils, chatelaines studded with pearls, and tight-waisted brocade gowns down which cascaded lace and jewels.

The luxury of Venezia dazzled even the shahs of Persia, grandees from Spain, India's maharajahs and noblemen from London to the Golden Horn. They paraded, too, in gilded sashes and exotic tunics, diamonded turbans and dolmans encrusted with gems.

Venice was profligate and voluptuous: over eleven thousand courtesans, celebrated for their beauty and proficiency, signaled their availability from gondolas lighted by red lanterns.

Once a year, a resplendent fleet reenacted the *sposalizio del mare,* the "wedding" of the Doge and the sea, to the fanfare of trumpets and the boom of cannons. The Doge sat on a golden throne in the Bucentaur, that gigantic galleon festooned with silken hangings and crimson pennants, which some 300 painted oars propelled. To this day, the spectacle commemorates the moment in 1177 when the Pope presented a ring of sovereignty to the Doge, who tossed it into the great lagoon to "marry" the Republic not to Rome but to the Adriatic Sea.

All these images tumbled through my mind that chilly, rain-drenched December day I stood in the prow of the *vaporetto* from the railway terminal.

My heart sank. This was no city sheathed in splendor. The palaces past which we chugged were mausoleums: silent, forbidding, shuttered tight. The grand facades were streaked and stained. The striped tethering poles for gondolas stood askew in the canals like clowns trapped in antic angles. The marble steps against which the waters lapped were slimy; the mansions wore hems of moldy green. . . .

For five days I explored a desolate city. I shivered across countless bridges and empty piazzas. The fabled square of San Marco, so beautifully paved in marble and trachyte, depressed me. The legendary basilica repelled me: a garish half-mosque, half–Roxy theater. The gold mosaics were scarcely visible, lost in the wintry shadows like gypsies hiding their gaudy beads.

I was so very young, and I lived as the naive and the unutterably romantic do: on the extremities of emotion, swinging from ecstasy to despair. Here, in this Xanadu I had so long dreamed of seeing, there was no ecstasy: all was dismal and wrapped in shrouds.

For five wretched days I ate in bars with steamy windows and shivered through grim museums. For five wretched nights I slept under clammy sheets. At times I fought down tears in that gray, all-embracing vapor, recalling Baedeker's warning about a noxious city of "malarial exhalations."

I had come to a ghostly place from which sensible people had fled. I felt foolish (no, cheated and embittered) to have journeyed so far and spent so much to find . . . an abandoned carrousel.

✟✟✟

Today I know that Venice repelled me not only because it was December and the city had drawn into a sullen shell, but because (like my dinner hostess) I was there alone. If there is one place on earth you should never, never see alone, it is Venice. Its romanticism magnifies your loneliness until beauty becomes unbearable. This fairyland that dazzles the summer senses can break your heart. In winter, a sense of sadness pervades so much expiring grandeur. I ached with the melancholy James Morris saw in these "lost purposes . . . crumbling masonries suffused in winter twilight."

Many years later, long after that disenchanted visit, I brought my bride to Venice. Uncertain of what she (or I) might find or truly feel, I sputtered cautious apologies: "You may not like it . . . it's gingerbread . . . pink Popsicle buildings . . . spun-sugar domes. . . ."

We left the train and walked down the platform,

thinking we might just as well be in Penn Station, and went through the doors. . . . The splendor of Venice in summer slammed against us.

I beheld a place I had never seen: pink palaces and alabaster pavilions, sparkling towers and spires, a profusion of pinnacles and cupolas and minarets. And all that jeweled scene was mirrored, doubling in the water, every tint and hue trailing toward us in shimmering ribbons.

We sank into a gondola and stretched low among the cushions. The up-curved prow of that singular craft cut into the air above us, a creature out of myth, and we were borne, floating, into an enfolding dream: Byzantine mansions, columns of porphyry and jasper, Gothic arches and Palladian domes. Everywhere flags, pennants, buntings fluttered; the gay tethering poles tilted at playful tangents.

Everything was ablaze with light: embroidered damask tossed across railings, canopies of colored canvas, a thousand streamers with heraldic emblems. Children's laughter trilled from bower windows and women sang from balconies laden with laundry and honeysuckle. On every side medallions and statues (ceramic angels and knights and saints in terra cotta) beguiled our vision. Occasional pines and poplars thrust up from hidden gardens to hint of green walks and pergolas dripping mimosa.

The beauty of Venice simply stunned us: the Rialto bridge, one graceful marble arch ninety feet long, the matchless Ca' d'Oro, the palace of the Foscaris, the Palazzo Rezzonico (where Browning died), and a riot of architectural conceits: Grecian pillars, Arabic ogee windows, Florentine crenelations.   *Cop. 1*

I glanced at my wife: tears had wet her cheeks. She was all wonder and gratitude—not to me but to Venice, for being there for her to see.

Our gondolier plied his long oar, stepping back and forth on his runway; his flat straw hat crimson banded with two girlish streamers and his jersey striped blue and white: the gondoliers' costume has not changed down the centuries. Small sea-horse brasses gleamed on each side of us, bitted and tasseled, as we glided through—a fantasy.

How strange that we saw a funeral cortège, the coffin within a black cabin on a barge followed by a string of black boats, on their way to the outer-island cemetery of San Michele. Our helmsman cried "Hoy!" and again a warning "Hoy!" as he swung us around a corner, skimming into a side canal where bartizane loomed above us.

That night, in the Gritti Palace, we heard micro-phones blare out a tenor's "Santa Lucia," then a contralto mooning the "Barcarole." We stepped onto our balcony. Against the velvet darkness we beheld lights and lanterns floating down the Grand Canal beneath us. A large vessel with an orchestra of mandolins and singers led a proces-sion: an armada of gondolas was tied to the barge's sides, and more gondolas drifted in the wake; a quartet at two microphones in a flickering spotlight caroled operatic cadenzas.

From all the gondolas people waved at us, and we laughed and cried, "Bravo! Bravo!" and applauded like children at a circus.

It was spangled hokum, I suppose, but so endearing: an Italian illustrated version of *A Thousand and One Nights.*

Venice is not a city; it is a caravansary. It is not a place, but a dream, a mystery of mansions, radiant with shifting rays of light—the sun, the moon—on iridescent waters.

The beauty of Venice was such that other cities sought uniqueness by adopting her name: Czarist St. Petersburg called itself "the Venice of the North"; Bangkok, "the Venice of the East"; Amsterdam, "a little Venice"; and in distant Venezuela, Maracaibo boasts of being "Venice on a lake."

Someone likened Venice to "a gorgeous, floating swan." To me it is a mirage, forever bewitching and bewitched.

To walk in Venice is sheer delight, for you are sure to get lost amidst the 118 islets, ringed by a maze of canals, where there are no less than three thousand streets, squares, and alleyways barely wide enough for two. And lost, you discover yet another enchanting bridge or piazza with unexpected trees and throngs of children, or a noisy marketplace where old sails serve as awnings, tipped to shade carts laden with fruit, flowers, hats, beads. Once, off the Campo Santa Margherita, I found a shorn bell tower and a Gothic entrance to an old convent with a new sign: CINEMA.

What fanciful names the Venetians chose for their fairyland: the Bridge of Paradise, the Way of Monkeys, the Filled-in Canal of Thoughts, the Lane of the Curly-Haired Woman, the Alley of the Proverbs, the Way of the Sword. I relish the nomenclature:

fondamenta	a broad quayside promenade
calle	a lane
ruga	a street with shops
piscina	once a pond
salizzada	a paved alley

—and a plentitude of *campos, rivas, cortes, campiellos.*

Down any canal, however cramped, scows transport wood, coal, raffia-bound caskets of wine, crated vegetables, bales of cloth—or mounds of garbage.

Everywhere, gondolas bob and skim across the waterways. No one knows what the name means, nor where it was born. Some philologists link "gondola" to a Turkish word, others to a Maltese; but most dictionaries of etymology simply say "origin obscure" or "probably Italian."

Some historians think the graceful craft came from ancient Phoenicia, or Carthage; others trace the six silvered prongs on the upswept prow (always six, for unknown reasons) to funeral barges on the Nile, or to a kind of canoe in China. I like the theory that *góndola* is a corruption of the Greek name for Charon's Ferry, which carried the dead (each corpse gripping a coin between its teeth as fare for the journey) to Hades, crossing the river Styx that seven times circles the netherworld.

There were 11,000 gondolas in Venice at the zenith of her power. A sixteenth century law decreed that every gondola must be black (why, I do not know) and they still are black, gleaming, varnished shells whose prows ride high out of the water like the beaks of strange birds yearning to fly.

The most astounding thing of all about Venice, of course, is where it *is*. This archipelago of alluvial isles, laced by marshy lagoons and a labyrinth of waterways, was where an ancient mainland tribe, the Veneti, periodically fled from Goths, Huns and marauding Lombards. The Veneti built crude shelters and huts in the morass, and later erected watchtowers for sentries and warning bells. The silted soil could not support much weight, but watchtowers were essential to survival, so the Veneti drove wooden pilings deep into the bogs of mud and sand and built their campanile.

How this swampy refuge grew, its people

pounding more and more tree trunks into the soggy soil, defies my comprehension. The huge Church of the Salute rests on 1,250,000 stilts. (It took thirty-four years to build.) The Cathedral of San Marco sits on a gigantic, subterranean forest. Every palace, every mansion, every huddled row of houses in Venice is supported by wooden pillars from the mainland, hammered into the silt.

I once asked an engineer how on earth such construction could endure. He smiled and said, "The massive edifices do not stand 'on earth'; indeed, Venice does not stand at all: it *floats*, held in place by an odd equilibrium of liquid and geological pressures."

I did not understand him.

⚓⚓⚓

The early Venetians had precious salt and saltfish to barter. By the tenth century the islanders had learned to conjure glass in marvelous forms and glazes: enameled goblets and topaz beakers, allegories etched into mirrors, agate flasks and bowls of millefiori. The candelabra and chandeliers of Venezia were so magnificent that they soon adorned churches and mosques, ballroom salons and royal boudoirs, throughout Europe and the Middle East.

Even more prized was Venetian *cristallo*: perfectly clear, thin, delicate glass such as had never before been seen. *Cristallo* could be duplicated nowhere, such dexterity and speed did its process require. So jealous was Venice of her monopoly that when a glassblower fled to the mainland, the Doges promptly sent assassins to find and kill him. Rarely did the slayers fail to accomplish their mission.

Venice became a mighty maritime power by building galleys and dromonds designed to be half-freighter, half-warship. Each vessel used a battalion of slaves who served as oarsmen, in harbors, and as warriors in battle. The ships had such skillful captains, such excellent and varied sails, that they could reach England (2,500 miles away) within a month.

Pirates swiftly learned to fear Venezia's fighting force. The Turks, despatching fleets of three to four thousand ships, often conquered some Venetian trading port or refitting isle. But the Arsenal of Venice developed a remarkable technique for pouring more and more vessels from her dry docks. A new galley would be towed into "a great street of water" on either side of which were houses from whose successive windows were thrust sails, chains, guns, bread, rope, casks of wine and water. Ships were fully equipped within two hours.

This process was cannily shown to visiting diplomats to demonstrate that, for all its festivals and frippery, Venice possessed the most sophisticated production line in the world. At one point forty-five new ships came from the Arsenal each day.

They sailed down the Adriatic, attacking forts and cities along the coast of Dalmatia, then moved into the Mediterranean, subjugating Cyprus, Crete, Morea (the Peloponnese), and established sea routes for trade or plunder eastward to Rhodes and the Hellespont, westward to Sicily and Iberia. In time the fleets of San Marco ventured beyond the pillars of Hercules, into the Atlantic, to Biscay, Normandy, Britain, the Netherlands, and even far-off Baltic ports. The galleys of the *Serenissima* sailed back to Venice from the Dardanelles with treasures which overland caravans had transported from the fabled East: Persia, Afghanistan, Hindustan and Cathay.

The broad Riva degli Schiavoni was piled high with riches: the warehouses of Venice bulged with precious spices, dyes, drugs; purple cloth from Tyre; Chinese lacquer, jade and silk; gems and ginger from India; blades and olive oil from Spain, German pewter, tapestries from Flanders, wool from Portugal; Russian ermine and English weavings; rubies from Burma and sapphires from Ceylon; sandalwood and teak from Siam. From Africa came copper, lapis lazuli, serpentine and chalcedony; cotton from Egypt, slaves from Abyssinia and Morocco. Between its trade and loot of war, Venice simply burst with wealth.

Thomas Coryat, who used the odd *nom de plume* "Peregrine of Odcombe," wrote a travel book in 1608, and what he said of Venice was:

> . . . this incomparable city, this most beautiful
> queen, this paradise, this rich diadem (of) Chris-
> tendom, of which the inhabitants may as
> proudly vaunt as . . . the Persians have of their
> Ormus: . . . if the world were a ring, then
> should (Venice) be the gem thereof.

But naval power alone could not account for the supremacy of a city-state no more than three miles long and scarcely two miles wide. In a marvel of diplomatic dexterity the doges ("dukes") outwitted Charlemagne by claiming to be a fiefdom of Byzantium, and thwarted Constantinople by saying Rome was their sovereign and protector. In fact, Venice belonged to neither and lied to both. She remained independent and impregnable, a hub of commerce and banking, a strategic sanctuary "poised between Christianity and Islam."

Rome needed Venetian sea power—especially during the Crusades—which the patricians of St. Mark's exploited with crafty deceptions. They made diplomatic deals with Constantinople to guarantee safe conduct to Christian pilgrims heading for the Holy Land. Then, serving as a safe embarkation point, Venice sold the Crusaders transportation down the Adriatic or across the Balkans through Ottoman domain. To each zealous horde of pilgrims, the Venetians sold food, water, salt—and her protection. The middleman between Rome and Constantinople made Venice the gateway to distant Jerusalem.

It is a remarkable fact that for a thousand years no revolution tore Venice apart, and no cabals overthrew the reigning patricians. Neither religious passions nor political strife disturbed the growth or peace of the city-state on the waters.

The rulers of Venice won the confidence of their merchants and lower orders by providing for them with care, entertaining them with marvelous spectacles, and establishing strong, secure government. Whatever his fortune or career, a Venetian aristocrat's first and foremost duty lay in loyalty to the Republic.

As far back as 1310, a Constitution employed these remarkable phrases to define the purpose of government:

> to preserve the liberty and peace of the subjects of the republic, and to protect them from the abuses of personal power.

That Constitution still warrants the admiration of political theorists. (It influenced, directly or through hearsay, Montesquieu and Locke, Voltaire and Jefferson.)

To guard against "abuses of personal power," the patricians contrived extraordinary measures. The ruling doge was elected by his peers "for life" to discourage factional intrigue. The nobility knew that prolonged tenure easily turns into tyranny, so the Senate cannily place quite *old* men on the ducal throne. (This gambit was used by the Vatican's elite, too.)

A network of unique prohibitions checked ducal power. No doge was allowed to leave Venice—for any purpose, personal or official. No doge could act without the concurrence of six members of the Council of Ten. No doge was even permitted to talk in private to any foreigner, even an ambassador. Every letter to or from a doge was first read by censors. Even the activities of a dogaressa were closely watched and severely curtailed.

The Council of Ten never relaxed its guard against possible demagogues outside the administration or possible traitors within it. The Council met in secret and acted with dispatch. They were feared—and respected—by every Venetian.

Arrests were made at midnight, to magnify their portent. Punishments were swift and dramatic. Criminals were blinded; thieves had their hands cut off; men who "spoke ill" of the Republic lost their tongues. (Such punition, dreadful to modern sensibility, was approved by the most pious of our ancestors.)

The torsos of traitors or conspirators (however illustrious) were found on many a morning, hanging upside down, by one leg, from the Gothic arches of Il Palazzo Ducale. As for petty malefactors, or priests caught in moral peccadillos, they were locked in open cages and suspended from the belfry of the old Campanile. Some were given bread and water; others simply starved and died in public view.

Prison cells lined the baking attics beneath the roof of the Doge's Palace, beyond the aptly named Bridge of Sighs, and gruesome *càrceri* lined the cellars. Every splash of a body dropped into a canal in the dark of night was credited to the Council.

Yet even the humblest citizen could realize that their rulers gave them precious order and security in a violent age. It was not "bread and circuses" which ensured the domestic tranquility of Venice; it was employment, safety and superb diversions.

⚜⚜⚜

We may relive the dazzling panoply of Venice for ourselves in the paintings of her artists: the brothers Bellini, who limned those remarkable portraits of doges; Veronese, with his sumptuous tableaux and gleaming costumes; Titian, who used courtesans with golden tresses as models for his voluptuous nudes; Tintoretto, with his singular palette of muted blues and greens; Canaletto, transfixed by the ever-changing light of the Grand Canal; Guardi, who caught the elegant frivolity of masquerading figures, outlined by slivers of silver, and made them mummers in some medieval allegory—and Vittore Carpaccio.

Carpaccio, I think, best sensed the vanity of

Venice. He saw the new Babylon as spectacle, and seized upon each detail of the sybaritic: brass trumpets and jade fans; pet monkeys, peacocks, exotic birds; zithers and lutes and exquisite flowers; palatial steps where toy dogs and shrewd cats recline in stately postures. Human freaks amused the Venetian fancy: dwarfs, hunchbacks, legless jesters—whom superstition endowed with the capacity to bring good fortune. Eunuchs and houris, Nubian pages and Ishmaelite slaves enliven the *dramatis personae*.

There is no mistaking a Carpaccio. He invested his lacquered canvases with a strange stillness, freezing time, as it were, for eternal remembrance.

The decline of Venice must have baffled the doges. Constantinople slowly drained Venetian trade and wealth, and when Vasco da Gama found a waterway around the Cape of Good Hope to India and the riches of the East, Venice was doomed.

It took three centuries for her dominion to die; and in that prolonged twilight, Venice danced to the music of desire, saturating her profligate senses, drifting, in Morris' words, "from power to luxury, from luxury to flippancy, from flippancy to impotence."

Napoleon conquered the *Serenissima* in 1799, and gave her to Austria, then Italy.

✝✝✝

All of that lies in the past. When I sit in the Piazza, sipping cappuccino or spooning an ice, listening to the concerts of Florian's orchestra or Quadri's band, watching the world's visitors gape across that glorious square Bonaparte called "the most beautiful drawing room in the world"—then the history of Venice is but a tapestry hung in the hall of memory.

The magnificent basilica was designed after the five-domed Church of the Holy Apostles which Justinian built, centuries earlier, in Constantinople. There are 40,000 square feet of mosaics in San Marco, and thousands of colored patterns glitter in the half-domes across the portals. Trumpeting angels march up and down the pinnacles which punctuate the immense facade, and four marvelous bronze horses rear on the middle balcony. They were looted from Constantinople in 1204.

Three buildings enclose the Piazza on three sides, and across their long rooflines a succession of statues (knights? cavaliers? nameless princes?) stands like sentinels in the sky. Each building is footed by a long arcade of shops; from each archway hangs a glass lantern, tinted mauve.

Swarms of pigeons dot the air, their beating wings dappling the light. The pigeons are especially loved by Venetians because, according to legend, their ancestors miraculously appeared with tiny gold crosses in their beaks to guide the terrified Franks to a haven on the marshes: the islet called Rivo Alto, from which "Rialto" comes.

The famous pink Campanile soars its crescendo into the sky. But this is not the true, old tower, where Galileo demonstrated the first telescope. That campanile crashed to the ground without warning over seventy years ago, and this one is a replica.

The Doges Palace is surely one of the most beautiful and surprising buildings in the world. The Gothic arches, ornamented with quartrefoil spaces, stand sunken and oddly squat. How can so massive an edifice be so delicate—and tantalizing? It is faced in pink, arranged in oblique patterns, with lovely balconies and Moorish windows and a superb balustrade.

As the sun strikes the golden, onion-shaped domes of the Cathedral and all the spires and belfries blaze like images of Golconda, my heart leaps for the glory spread before me.

But I must be fair to those, like the hostess with whose antipathy I began this essay, who think Venice a campy, tinseled tourist trap. Here is my least happy memory: One night, I signaled our gondolier to take us into a narrow side-canal. He moaned, *"Signor!"* and put two fingers to his nose; but my wife laughed and I waved him on.

He raised his eyes to heaven for forgiveness and swung us around a corner.

The water was flat, silent and stinking. We moved between tenements with scabrous doors. Here and there, naked light bulbs revealed dismal rooms: a sweating man in an undershirt, a slattern dumping garbage. We heard the sad, furtive sounds of night: creakings, coughings, a groan, a whisper, a startling slap to still a crying child. In this fetid water alley, not twelve feet wide, I recalled Thomas Mann's images of the plague in *Death in Venice,* and remembered that malaria had killed Dante here.

I appealed to our gondolier queasily. He smirked, shouted "Hoy!" and oared us into the wide, clean Giudecca. A breeze—so fresh and sweet I could not believe it—touched my face.

⚓⚓⚓

You must go to the Lido, that narrow spit of land which protects Venice from the Adriatic—not to see the posh hotels or beach cluttered with cabanas, but to ride back on a *vaporetto.* If you do this at twilight, you will behold the panorama of Venezia, mirrored in colored, dancing waters, quivering in the silken mystery of her beauty.

This Xanadu will disappear; all the shining palaces are sinking, sinking into the great lagoon, and there will be nothing like Venice again.

SNAPSHOTS: Around the World in Thirty Scenes

"Paris." Does the Eiffel tower leap into your mind? The Arc de Triomphe? Notre Dame? Not into mine. What I see is the gilded statue of Joan of Arc in the minuscule Place des Pyramides.

This effigy is certainly not the most interesting statue in the world, and far from the best in Paris. But I always think of the golden damsel on her golden horse, proudly displaying her golden banner, because the very first night I saw Paris, when I was twenty-one, an ebullient Frenchman named Maurice marched me down the dark arcades of the Rue de Rivoli, pointed to the statue, and exclaimed: "John Dark!"

"Who?"

"John *Dark*. The Maid of Orleans. The savior of France. The—"

"Oh, Joan of Arc!"

"*Oui!* A great, great woman!" Maurice snapped into a military brace and saluted. I, determined to respect every smidgeon of the native mores, joined him. We stood in reverent paralysis for a moment.

Maurice lowered his hand, sighing, "You know, she died a virgin!" That, he implied, was why the French had put up the statue to her.

Or take bewitching "San Francisco." Do you think of cable cars? The Golden Gate? Chinatown? Not I. I hear the radio-station tag line: "You are listening to KABL in San Francisco, the city of unpretentious charm."

Now, a slogan like that might sound spiffy for

Naples, the city of unpretentious smells, or New London, the hatchery of unpretentious submarines. But San Francisco?! Shucks, by now that toy metropolis ought to be sophisticated enough to scorn such trumpery as "unpretentious charm."

Or take "Pisa." Does that name trigger the image of the Leaning Tower? Not to me. When I hear "Pisa" the snapshot that leaps into my mind is—a camel. The startling sight of a camel near the Leaning Tower of Pisa buried itself in the "miscellaneous" drawer of my mental files, where it remained—unfulfilled, but minding its own business—until I learned that back in the seventeenth century an Italian soldier brought a few camels to his native land. He had taken them as loot after a battle against the Turks. They (the camels) married, had babies, and their progeny seem perfectly at home in Pisa.

I'm sure you can see that my brain has a way of making ludicrous associations. My mind latches on to one scene or sound or episode that typifies a place forever after.

Take Miami Beach. That salubrious resort has a hundred gaudy attractions, but *I* think of it as the locale for the dear old dowager who said, "These shoes? I use them only for street walking."

Such petrified memories may strike you as pretty peculiar. But what can I do? Here is a sampler of the indefensible snapshots that flash onto the screen of my mind whenever I read or hear the names of certain places:

Las Vegas

Not the flaming heat, the blazing sidewalks, the icy hotel rooms. Not the housewives lined up at slot machines, dropping dimes and quarters in cat-atonic dreams of fortune. Not the ten-gallon hats and cowboy boots of ranchers, nor the fringed leather skirts of their "womenfolk." Not the se-quined beach slippers around the gigantic pools. Not even the insane incongruity of desert hostels aping Persian palaces or the mosques of Istanbul. What I see is one demure ad in a local paper: *WEDDING GOWNS FOR ALL OCCASIONS.*

Tel Aviv

An American tourist picked up the phone in his hotel room and asked for a bottle of 7-Up.

The switchboard operator answered in a charm-ing accent: "7-Up? Yes, *sir!*"

The beverage never arrived; but the next morn-ing the tourist was awakened precisely at seven o'clock.

Moscow

A tongue-in-cheek advertisement in *Krokodil,* whose weekly satire is as rare as it is risky in the Paradise of Workers, Farmers and Party Bureau-crats:

WANTED
Typist—to copy Top Secret documents.
Must be unable to read.

Paris

We dined in grand style at Pruniers, as we do whenever we are in Paris. My wife pointed to the first dessert listed on that renowned menu:

Cheesecake: American specialty, based
on recipe of Lindy's in New York.

Burford

In the lounge of an old inn in the Cotswolds, not far from Chipping Norton and Upper Slaughter, I browsed through a country weekly. One item still haunts me: a letter addressed to the Dean of the Augustinian Order in Guisborough, England, had been returned to its sender with the address crossed out and this correction written by some local minion in Her Majesty's Royal Post Office:

This monastery was
dissolved in 1540.

Tokyo

A Japanese gentleman in a kimono and a Western fedora clattered up to me on his *getas* ("clogs"), grinning. The flash of steel in his mouth almost blinded me. He jerked downward in the *de rigueur* bow and giggled: "Ah, prease. I speak En-grish. A*rr*ow me. . . ." (The Japanese seize every chance to "plactice" their "Engrish.") He held up a cigarette.

I
No, thank you.

JAPANESE GENTLEMAN
Ah, so. . . . But I desire . . . prease . . . one *match*. For cigallette.

I
Ahh, so!

As I struck a match I remembered a story I had heard from a U.S. Navy officer who hailed a taxi in Tokyo. He spoke not a word of Japanese. He uttered the name of his hotel, in English, and the driver beamed, nodded, giggled, but made no move to drive on. He just blinked incomprehension.

The officer reached for a cigarette; lighting it, he noticed he was using a matchbook from his hotel. Banzai! He leaned closer to the driver and displayed the matchbook, tapping his finger on the cover.

The cabdriver grinned and nodded. *"Hai!"* he barked. (Even the most porcelain Nipponese maiden utters the affirmative with a bark.) Off zoomed the taxi.

When the brakes finally squealed and the cab stopped, the driver turned to the officer with a flourish of the hand.

The Navy officer opened the door—and

flinched. He was at the entrance to a match factory. It was, indeed, the very factory which made matches for his hotel: its address was what the officer had so cleverly tapped.

Martha's Vineyard

The gingerbread hotel has a gingerbread porch traipsing prissily around it, and the gingerbread windows overlook the picturesque harbor of Edgartown. Friends were amazed to learn that my wife and I would stay there. One summer islander said, "There must be fifty rocking chairs on that porch! And all day long, old fuddy-duddies just sit there and rock back and forth, back and forth."

I could hardly wait to join the fuddy-duddies. Each morning I would hide behind the *Vineyard Gazette* to conceal what I am: a shameless eavesdropper. One fine forenoon I was rewarded beyond my deserts.

Scene: The porch.

Aging gentleman occupies one rocker. White flannels, blue blazer, straw hat, pince-nez. His eyes: blue water. His skin: soil erosion.

Enter septuagenarian lady. Pink cheeks, pink hair, pink parasol, pink purse, pink peekaboo blouse, pink furbelows and farthingale, for all I know.

WHITE FLANNELS

Good morning, Mathilda.

PINK LADY

Good morning, Theobald.

WHITE FLANNELS

Heard from your daughter?

PINK LADY

Long letter this morning. (Sits.) She writes that
she and John just *threw* away the guidebooks and
struck out on their own. Drove everywhere. Off
the beaten paths. They simply took any road or
turn that caught their fancy.

WHITE FLANNELS

Good heavens! In *India?*

PINK LADY

Mmh. They *are* adventurers. Emily says they
drove into one *dear* little village, a place with an
unpronounceable name—

WHITE FLANNELS

Most are.

PINK LADY

—while the natives—Hindus, I presume—

WHITE FLANNELS

Probably.

PINK LADY

—were all in a quaint little temple, worshipping
some ancient deity—

WHITE FLANNELS

Fancy that!

PINK LADY

—and when the natives emerged from the temple, and saw Emily—you *know* how very blonde
and fair she is—

WHITE FLANNELS

Oh, yes, *very*.

PINK LADY

—they *flung* themselves at her feet! Why, they
took her for a goddess!

WHITE FLANNELS (stops rocking)

Took her for a *godd*ess?

PINK LADY

For a goddess.

WHITE FLANNELS

How nice.

They rock in unison, seeing India.
The ghost of Kipling cackled in my ear.

Berlin

The morning papers are very good—and un-
nerving: pedantic, political, fractious, crushingly
erudite. Yet glints of cynicism are sprinkled
through the chronicles. And humor.

The Germans are not reputed to possess much
humor. Satire, yes, especially in the acid-sharp

cartoons. How delightful, then, to read this item, reproduced from Hamburg's solemn *Die Zeit:*

> A sign in a students' dormitory in Sweden reads:
> "Italians are not allowed to sing after midnight."
> "Germans are not permitted to get up before 5 A.M."

There's a semester of anthropology crammed into those lines.

Chicago

Wandering around the Loop one day, along the streets off Randolph, "Chicago's Rialto," whose movie theaters and restaurants captivate countless conventioneers (and half the farm folk of the Middle West), I saw this legend on a second-storey window across the avenue:

"STAIRWAY TO STARDOM"
BELLY-DANCE STUDIO

I leaned against a lamppost, hoping to catch a glimpse of at least one aspiring belly dancer entering or leaving the premises—perhaps the voluptuous Queen of Belly Dancers herself, once the Toast of Marrakesh, stranded in Chicago and driven to the extremity of teaching her noble art to buck-teethed girls from Milwaukee or ambitious tarts from the bordellos around Twenty-second Street.

My vigil was in vain. The only mortal to mount the "Stairway to Stardom" was a bald-headed oaf who walked as if his ankles had recently been broken. He had no belly to speak of.

Some nights, when I find it hard to fall asleep, I flick the magic lantern in my head to replace the hairless oaf with Scheherazade, diaphanous in veils and sheer pantaloons and upturned slippers from Byzantium.

Oxford

Lubricating my larynx in a pub, I ran across this item in the *Spectator:*

> A young British surgeon, on his first visit to America, was invited to look up a cystoscope (an instrument for viewing the inside of the bladder). To his astonishment, he saw the sign: "Visit Joe's Bar!"
>
> For a moment the young surgeon thought he was beholding the final extremity of a national mania for advertisement. Then he moved the instrument, and saw that he was gazing at a segment of a plastic cocktail stick.
>
> How it got there remains a mystery.

Kowloon

From Hong Kong, each morning, we rode the Star ferry to Kowloon, across that incredible harbor filled with sampans, where whole families live and eat and sleep, propelled by slender Chinese women with sleek black hair and black mandarin jackets and trousers, plying the long oar with a baby slung across their backs.

Each noon I lunched with my wife at Kowloon's renowned Peninsula Hotel, a Victorian haven of overhead fans and bamboo chairs and broad porches with latticed balustrades. British ladies and gentlemen have favored the Peninsula for a century, its cool salons and reading rooms populated by characters out of Maugham or Noël Coward. We drank sherry and munched cold cucumber sandwiches on very thin brown bread, followed by iced tea, faultlessly served by graceful silent waiters from Indonesia.

But what I remember most vividly about exotic Kowloon is this sign in a tailor shop:

CUSTOMERS GIVING ORDERS
WILL BE
SWIFTLY EXECUTED

Santa Monica

The cliffs loomed above me as I lay on the sand, and palm trees paraded across the cerulean skyline. Behind me, the beach mansions of Goldwyn, Zanuck, Warner—walled-off from hoi polloi—glistened in the sun. The greatest of these pleasure domes was William Randolph Hearst's, and if you pulled yourself up the enclosing wall you saw his white palace, fronted by a swimming pool fit for

Olympians, spanned by a marble bridge. There were eighty telephones inside Mr. Hearst's (and Miss Marion Davies') dream pavilion. . . .

I heard a woman shouting. I sat up. On the shore, a fat woman was waving her arm and crying, "Come out, Sandra! Come *out!*"

A girl of seven or eight waded back through the wavelets. "Mother!" she pouted. "Can't I stay in the water until my lips turn blue?"

Madrid

A movie theater. The marquee advertised *Jennie,* starring Jennifer Jones and Joseph Cotten, with this banner:

> "*Qué es el tiempo? Qué es espacio? Una eterna pregunta, un misterio, una ilusión, una fatalidad.*"

which means:

> "What is time? What is space? An eternal question, a mystery, an illusion, a necessity of fate."

You won't find a marquee like that in Schenectady.   *you will now!*

Jamaica

On a Caribbean cruise, we sailed into the steaming port of Kingston. It is an ugly, blistering city. Shriveled by the humid, horrid heat, I ordered a cold Silver Fizz, a humectant made of rum and ambrosia. Soon, uplifted, I scanned the *Jamaican Star*. God's mercy sent my eyes directly to this tale:

Turn Back, Foolish Girl, Turn Back!

Miss Blossom Mae Jetheroe, 23, was sentenced to seven days in gaol for "accosting" gentlemen on King Street. In passing sentence, Mr. Justice Cecil Horstcroft sternly admonished the errant female: "The wages of sin is surely *death*. O shameless, foolish girl, mend your ways!"

Yes, yes, Blossom Mae, listen to your just sentencer! Wrest your tinkling feet from the primrose path! Spurn those tawdry escapades that imperil your very soul! Stray not from the straight and narrow!

Think, Miss Blossom Mae! Turn back! There still is time! Let the blush of virtue return to your still young cheeks!

I have been infatuated with Jamaican prose ever since.

Venice

Far from the splendor of San Marco, far from the palaces of the Grand Canal, I wandered into a lane, decrepit and malodorous. An old nameplate, long since tarnished, caught my eye. The plaque was attached to a warped, faded-blue door that hung from hinges eaten by rust. The letters on the escutcheon were worn down by decades of polishing. I had to step close to decipher what once had been an illustrious sign:

MARCO POLO
UFFICIO TURISTICO AGENZIA

The phrases from *Ozymandias* swarmed into my mind.

Nantucket
  Scene: The porch of an old inn.
  Enter, old New England lady, in erect disdain. Takes rocking chair near mine. Nods to me. Opens reticule. Lace handkerchief. Violet sachet. Begins to rock, gazing at the sea.
  Enter, second old New England biddy.

SECOND O.N.E.B.
(spying first O.N.E.B.)

Ah, my dear Mrs. Prksmm!

FIRST O.N.E.B.

Good morning, Mrs. Bntrkp. *Do* sit here.

SECOND O.N.E.B.

Thnkyu . . .

FIRST O.N.E.B.

And *did* you visit with the Agrlnts last night?

SECOND O.N.E.B.

Oh, yes. . . . Indeed. . . . Indeed, yes. . . . *Lovely* visit.

FIRST O.N.E.B.

Mmh. And how is dear Vrnca?

SECOND O.N.E.B.

Middling.

FIRST O.N.E.B.

And Charles? *Dear* Charles . . .

SECOND O.N.E.B.

We-ell . . .

(sighs)

FIRST O.N.E.B.

I know. . . . Did he not used to think himself a
beagle?

SECOND O.N.E.B.

Mm-hm. . . . Still does.

FIRST O.N.E.B.

Pity . . .

Chelsea

I wandered into Chelsea Town Hall, on Ken-
sington High, and beheld this marble tablet on a
wall:

To The Memory of
George Henry, Fifth Earl of Cadogan
Seeing in Rank an Obligation, in Possessions
a Trust, and in Duties a Privilege, he Sought
Steadfastly the Good of Chelsea, where his
Name is held in Grateful Remembrance.

Is there lovelier English anywhere, or so noble a tribute?

New Orleans

Near the overwrought-iron balconies of the French Quarter, waiting for a Streetcar named Despair, I could not help overhearing this exchange between two fetching Southern "bills" (belles), in the honeyed patois of the South:

FIRST BELLE

Wha, Josiph jes' happens t' be onea mah *favrit* min. 'Mimber hem?

SECOND BELLE

Yi-is! Ah mit hem win Ah was et yaw Aunt Shollit's potty!

FIRST BELLE

The tom you taw the him on thit purty yalla frock?

SECOND BELLE

Yi-is! Sech a *lovely* dre-ess—but *Lawd,* Ah had t' fond sex pens to pen up thet him bifaw Ah c'd show mah *face* at th' potty.

Zurich

In picturesque old Zurich, which resembles a sugarplum illustration for a fairy tale and is about as picturesque as you can get without cloying your tonsils, a tiny old *hausfrau* stopped, scrutinized me, nodded briskly, stepped closer, and asked, "Do you understand German?"

"*Etwas,*" I winced. (German is better suited to glowering than wincing.)

She drew herself up. "So what do you think of my daughter-in-law?!"

"*Bitte?*"

"You know what she did? I'll tell you what she did, *geehrter Herr,* and tell me if you don't agree that it is one of the most dis*gus*ting things you ever heard a daughter-in-law do. I was in the kitchen, just keeping her company, mind you, not even *hinting*, by word or expression, what a mean, selfish wife she is to my son—a man who is an angel, an absolute *angel!*—when in the middle of *nothing*, she raises the chopping knife and says, 'Hannah, you look like a monkey!' " The little dowager fixed me with the glare of an Ancient Mariness. "So? What do you think?"

"Well . . ." I stammered.

"*Danke schön!*" she cackled. "A monster! An *echt* monster . . . I knew from your kind features that you would agree! *Auf wiedersehen!*"

She waved and vanished into an agglutination of Zurichian gnomes.

Bloomsbury

Scene: My room.

Enter a Coldstream Guard, in mufti: waistcoat, striped trousers, regimental tie, bowler, spats.

Trimly moustached. Ramrod spine. Carries the inevitable, impeccable umbrella.

"Mr. Rstn?" He strangles the vowels inside the dungeon of his nose.

"Quite." I go British to the core.

The Coldstream Guard snaps his fingers.

Enter an alpaca jacket, unpressed trousers, shoes last shined during the reign of Ethelred the Unready. Encased in the alpaca is a waxy varlet, carrying a typewriter.

The Guardsman points to my writing table.

The yeoman steps forward, deposits the machine, mumbles uncalled-for apologies, and vanishes through the door.

Coldstream Guard (clicking his heels): *"Quite* shaw you'll find everything satisfactory, Mr. Rstn. Good-day!"

And that, friends of the Wilma P. Liederkranz Home for Wayward Maidens, is how a typewriter I rented was delivered to my digs in dear London town.

Kyoto

The singing floor.

As I walked along the wooden porch of the palace of Nijojo, little jewel of the once-mighty Shoguns, all around me nightingales sang. I paused; instantly, the nightingales stopped. I moved on; at once, the twitterings resumed.

Were hidden nightingales watching me from

some secret perch, secure when I moved and apprehensive when I stopped?

No. It was the *floor* that sang. Under pressure, the planks rub against hidden pegs to produce a melodious squeak like the cheeping of nightingales.

Did the Shoguns want their balcony to sing because they were so enamored of nightingales? No, again. The planks were cunningly designed to warn the nabobs of Japan when someone approached. Singing floors made it impossible for an assassin to catch a Shogun or his guards asleep.

I have strolled inside the White House a dozen times, and in the Palais Elysée, and in the corridors of Parliament (Buckingham Palace never invited me in), and even in Chicago's hallowed City Hall; but in none of these bastions of power did I ever hear a sparrow, much less a nightingale, herald my eminent imminence.

Only the Shoguns fear me, and they are deaf in their graves.

Beverly Hills

Deep, deep in the sleep of an accomplished somniac, I felt a feathery poke in the shoulder and dimly heard my little boy's voice: "Dad . . . wake up. . . . The house across the street. . . . It's on fire! . . . Engines . . . firemen . . ."

I clawed up the cotton ladder of consciousness.

I listened. The night was hushed, serene and soundless. I made a mental note to cut my son out of my will. "Having a nightmare?" I muttered.

"Dad!" exclaimed the injured lad. "Come look."

I tottered to the window. I pried open my eyelids. *Flames,* by God! Big, red tongues of fire licking away at the roof of the house of the movie star who lived across the street. And two big, shiny fire engines. And nozzles spitting foam from hoses spread around like tangled octopi. And firemen running around busily—on tiptoe.

Directing this singular tableau was the Fire Chief of Beverly Hills, signaling his helmeted yeomen hither and thither—in pantomime. I swear it: he was cautioning his gallant crew not to make undue plebeian noises. Damnedest scene I ever saw. Gilbert and Sullivan. No noise is permitted to ruffle the night in Lollipop Lane. Let naught disturb the sleeping kings of never-never land. Not even during a real, honest-to-god fire. Even the splash of water from the hoses was *pianissimo,* a tone poem by Debussy.

"Good night, son."

I returned to my bed, where I made a mental note to take the lad to see the Rams play the Washington Redskins that very Sunday.

Jerusalem

We were driving in the blistering heat from Tel Aviv to Jerusalem, and as I read a road sign, "Gaza

. . . Beersheba . . . Eilat," a disembodied head swam into view just beyond the open window of our moving car. A wide-brimmed, very black hat sat on the head, and long _payess_ ("sidelocks") and a black beard were beneath it. Then the beard and _payess_ fluttered in the wind, together almost horizontal. A Hebrew prophet drifted past me—calm as a cucumber—on a motorbike.

"And the Lord shall give them wings . . ."

Nara

Walking toward the great five-roofed pagoda, I was overtaken by a breathless, buck-toothed gentleman in a kimono who jerked into the obligatory bow, giggled and hissed: _"Ssss!_ I speak Engrish!"

ROSTEN

Delighted.

GIGGLES

Ssss! You rike Jopon?

ROSTEN

I like Japan very much.

GIGGLES

Ah, _sso!_ . . . Joponese people enjoy basuboru. You rike basuboru?

ROSTEN

Yes, I like . . . baseball.

GIGGLES
Ssss! . . . Plaps you have opinion on Weary Maze?

ROSTEN
(with feeling)
Willie Mays may be the greatest baseball player who ever lived!

GIGGLES
(in ecstasy)
Prease, what is you busyness?

ROSTEN
I am a writer. And what, sir, is yours?

GIGGLES
I teach Engrish.

Istanbul

Fists. Fists pounding on automobile doors. It's illegal to blow your horn in Istanbul (at night you blink your headlights) so Istanbul's drivers stick their left arms out of the windows and bang away furiously on the door panels. The first time I took a taxi, I thought we were being machine-gunned . . .

My English friend was banging away on his Austin as we wove through the traffic along the Bosphorus. (Here, says Greek mythology, is where the goddess Io, turned by Jupiter into a bull, swam across the channel. It grieves me to tell you that euphonious "Bosphorus" means "bull's passage.")

We glided past the minarets of the Ortaköy Mosque, the magnificent Dolmabahçe Palace, and Asia Minor lay shining across the strait. As we curved north, up into the hills, my host kept looking at his wristwatch. "Must get back before sundown."

"Appointment?" I asked.

"No . . . it's just . . . well, no one in his right mind wants to get caught on this road after sunset."

"Bandits?"

"N-no. Army installation. . . . Last year, a foreign couple—driving here after dark—were stopped, and abducted by some Turkish soldiers." He paused. "Both of them 'served' the regiment . . . for three days and nights."

His pretty wife laughed, a bit harshly. "Istanbul. . . . When we arrived, I wanted a driver's license. The police commissioner was horrified. 'A woman? Drive? *Alone?* No, no!—that is too foolish. You will be attacked!' "

" 'Nonsense. I have a scream that can . . .'

" 'Oh, no, no, *no,* dear lady! The one thing you must *not* do is scream. That would bring men running from all directions. Better to be raped by only one.' "

The Louvre

It is colossal in size, stupendous in content, the largest warehouse of art in the world. And it has brass grilles in its salon floors. To me, those ducts are the most precious of all the Louvre's treasures . . .

It was a cold, wet, bone-chilling November. Each day my shoes went soggy from sleet or rain. Each afternoon the frigid dampness had soaked through my hat, my coat, my jacket, my sweater, my shirt.

That was when I discovered the brass grilles in the floors of the Louvre. I stood over them, feet spread wide, feeling the blessed heat from unseen furnaces blow up my trousers. I opened my raincoat and loosened my belt to lure the heavenly warmth across my chest and arms and neck. And astride those miraculous ducts, I feasted my eyes, in unique ecstasy, on the paintings on the walls.

From my first grille, I beheld the *Mona Lisa*. My casement of skin rose, by my reckoning, to a blissful seventy-six degrees. From the instant of such lunatic calculation, I found myself grading the masterpieces according to my cutaneous temperature. Renoir's *Gabrielle* rated a salubrious 74; Brueghel's *Beggars* gripped my thoughts—and heated my bones to a glowing 72; Rembrandt, Raphael, Delacroix won a rapturous 70–76 any day of the week.

The Louvre (it means "magnificent house") was a fortress back in the twelfth century. Upon its remains, Francis I erected a new palace. Richelieu collected art for the Louvre right and left. Napoleon crammed the great halls with a gallimaufry of plunder from Egypt and most of Europe.

What *I* want to know is the name of the genius who designed the heating system.

Piccadilly

I raise my hand and solemnly swear that I overheard this exchange on a bus in Piccadilly between two Cockney ladies:

> FIRST WOMAN
> (nodding)
> Loiked the show, did she now?

> SECOND WOMAN
> Called it *smashing*.

> FIRST WOMAN
> Fancy that. A ply by Shikespeare. . . . Which one was it, luv?

> SECOND WOMAN
> I'nt sure, but I *think* it was "The Timing of the Screw."

Vienna

We drifted along the Ringstrasse, passed the baroque gem of the Opera, and turned toward Thérèse's favorite coffeehouse.

I loved the cafés of Vienna, those gleaming emporia of leisure where one could dally away the hours: reading papers from every capital in Europe, sipping coffee in twenty different brews and blends, sampling pastries from burnished-brass trolley carts: cakes and tarts and tortes, delicacies filled with custard of marzipan. And the *croissants*. . . !

It was Thérèse who informed me that this tour de force of the baker's art was not born in Paris. The *croissant* first appeared in Vienna back in 1683, when the ferocious Ottomans were besieging the Queen of the Danube. Some patriotic baker shaped a breakfast roll into a crescent, Islam's sign, and the shape captured the fancy of the beleaguered city, whose inhabitants went on a *croissant* binge in a wave of symbolic revenge.

"You see, *Liebchen*," Thérèse murmured, her tongue licking blobs of whipped cream off her rosy lips, "zince ve vere afraid ve could not beat ze monsters uf Islam, ve *ate* zem."

Whenever she bit into a *croissant*, she thought of Muhammed.

Kurashiki

My three Japanese colleagues stared at each other, and burst into hysterical laughter. Why? All I had done was ask, "Does any of you know of a barber near here?"

Came the high-pitched, shrill, laughter. That was all.

That night, I asked our American conference leader, who was soggy with know-how in the ways of Nippon, what on earth had caused the idiotic cachinnation. He shrugged. "You asked a question to which the answer probably was 'No.' "

"So?"

"But a Japanese *can't* say 'No.' That would be a terrible insult to you. So, embarrassed, he goes into giggles."

I mulled this over. "Well, how do you go about asking a question?"

He shrugged. "You could have said something like, 'Gentlemen, I am sure that men of your intellectual attainments would not possibly burden your formidable minds with so petty, so trifling a fact as . . . whether there is a barber nearby.' See?"

"No."

"Well, if your Japanese friends *don't* know if there's a barber around, they beam and bow and smile, 'Ah-*so*, yes, you are right, Rosten-san! We do not know of a barber.' But if one of them *does* know, he can cry, 'Such great surprise, Rosten-san! Just happens I *do* know of nearby barber! Is an honor beyond my wildest expectations to inform you of its humble location!' "

Hmmm. Yes, we have no bananas.

Lisbon

Down many a broad avenue in sun-drenched Lisbon, the pretty trolleys slowly roll. They roll slowly because layer upon layer of passengers hang onto the sides, clutching windows, posts, railings, handles, clawing at each other, crawling on each other, locking hands and legs around any reachable arm, neck, sleeve, head, tie, belt or coat, briefcase or purse or parcel.

I often stared at those frantic hordes of human barnacles. Something about the insane swarms puzzled me: for although the outsides of all the trolley cars were engorged, the interiors—no one ever *stood* inside a Lisbon trolley. Every seat was occupied, but the aisles were totally empty: no strap hangers, no pole holders, no vertical bipeds reading papers . . .

I could hardly wait to ask my friend Jorge to explain this absurd juxtaposition of inner space and outer chaos. He said, "It is the law."

"What law?"

"To stand in inside of *trole carro* is not allow."

"Why not?"

Jorge looked at me with pity. *"Amigo,* if many persons stand in the within—*poof! pop!*—the *carro* will break open in the central!"

I said I had never heard of a streetcar cracking open in the central under the weight of passengers in the within—*poof! pop!* or any other way.

"No?" he frowned.

"No."

He scratched his head. "Still, must be." Jorge spread out his tolerant arms and patient palms. *"Must* be, *amigo.* For if is not, *why would be such law?!"*

It was circular argument's finest hour.

O, ROYAL PAVILION!

In Xanadu did Kubla Khan
A stately pleasure-dome decree:
Where Alph, the sacred river ran
Through caverns measureless to man
Down to a sunless sea . . .
It was a miracle of rare device,
A sunny pleasure-dome with caves of ice . . .
Weave a circle round him thrice,
And close your eyes with holy dread,
For he on honey-dew hath fed,
And drunk the milk of Paradise.

If you take the train from London but fifty miles to Brighton, you will behold the fantastic Royal Pavilion, inspired (presumably) by Coleridge's hypnotic images. The pleasure-dome is a Hindu-Chinese-Persian-Islamic confection that will either captivate or outrage you. It has been called bewitching, absurd, elegant, barbarous, exotic, execrable, delicious, deplorable, romantic and ridiculous. I love it.

Some scholars sneer that the Royal Pavilion is *not* a rendition of the jeweled mansion of Kubla Khan. They say the flamboyant nonsense is modeled after the Jumma Musjid in Delhi, or the Taj Mahal. I see no reason to quibble. But the architecture pales beside the ghosts who haunt those gleaming corridors, and the tales that are told about that profligate Prince of Wales who built his bizarre dream palace before he became King George IV.

☐   ☐

✞✞✞

Brighton, a gay Channel resort, was a carnival of "bathing-machines" and gambling casinos, circuses and sideshows. The pleasure spa was famed among London's swells for its horseraces and favored for its orgies. A jaded nobility diverted itself with gala balls and fencing matches and "jingling contests," in which one or another rake, dressed in bells, dashed around blindfolded revelers who tried to catch him by following his tinklings.

They drank and danced and fornicated around the clock in Brighton. Raffish cavaliers cavorted with lavishly costumed ladies in *"elegant* and *decent* gallantry,"* one observer noted, italics and all, "however deranged they may be by convivial excess." They don't write like that anymore.

Brighton boasted of its therapeutic waters: a Dr. Awister's lotion of seawater and milk, and the sulphurous baths of a Hindu named Sake Deen Mahomed. The gent who bore this moniker was a first-class charlatan. He administered fierce massages after immuring his clients in noxious vapors scented with Oriental perfumes. "The Shampooing Surgeon," as he was called, festooned his clinic with a forest of crutches said to have been discarded by ecstatic patients cured of lumbago, gout or rheumatism. But some of the clientele he claimed to have healed had never heard of him, and others had never been within gunshot of Brighton. Mahomed himself lived to 101.

England's dissolute dandies, and their retinue of mistresses, used to nip down to Brighton for "the baths" and the gay parties of George Augustus Frederick, Prince of Wales. This carnal scion had bought himself a house in Brighton, which thereby became a "royal residence"—a haven for French refugees, Russian princesses, Indian potentates, Italian "macaronies," and beauteous mulattoes from the West Indies. "Brighton" became a synonym for folly.

The Prince, lampooned in countless doggerels, was

> In the course of one revolving moon,
> Jockey, actor, coachman and buffoon.

For twenty-two years, the fat, licentious Prince (at sixteen he sighed, "I am too fond of women and wine") built his gorgeous Pavilion. He hired and fired one architect after another, until the incomparable Nash put his signature to the work. The luxurious bonbon outraged both the local populace and hordes of gaping "trippers." It still does. It is so utterly un-*English,* a chunk of cheesecake fit for Disneyland. I love it.

How can I do justice to its onion domes and ogee windows, its Moghul minarets and Manischewitz finials? That delirious facade belies the

radiant interior: lanterns from Cathay and bamboo from Cambodia, damasked walls and blue-
gold draperies, a smashing saloon with little pa-
godas and *étagères* under a chandelier which is a
massive fountain of crystal. In the banquet room,
the reeling guests could choose from 116 culinary
concoctions, prepared by a French chef even Versailles envied.

The vast kitchen must be seen to be believed:
a mélange of painted iron palm trees dripping
painted iron leaves. The bedrooms beyond a delicate double stairway are a symphony of red lacquer and cerulean blues, tulip lamps, golden casements, Chinese screens and Persian panels.

The Royal Pavilion climaxed that craze for Orien-
talism which swept England after the Napoleonic
wars. India enflamed the vision of Shelley and
Byron *(Indian Serenade)*; and the Prince of Wales,
mesmerized by all he heard and read, translated
his dreams into his tinseled mansion in unlikely
Brighton. I love it.

George Augustus Frederick was an egomaniac,
dowsed in finery, and in love with uniforms. He
collected dressing gowns "of riotous colors," in
which he received diplomats, friends, and God
knows how many ambitious ladies of the court or
the brothel. He wore cockaded hats and golden
wigs, frogged cloaks with huge fur collars. He was
always "painted, scented and powdered." His

hulk was strapped into corsets and brocade waist-coats, high ruffs and tight, silk breeches. His military jackets were embroidered in gold and laden with immense epaulets. He even dressed in Scottish kilts—whether to please the Scots or soothe his vanity, I cannot say. He was "a colossal cocoon." He commissioned more portraits of himself than any monarch in history and sent his likeness, unasked, to every sovereign in Europe.

He was a paragon (or parody) of self-indulgence. He never got out of bed until six—in the afternoon. Servants opened his shutters at seven each morning, whereupon he breakfasted in bed, scanned a newspaper or letter, and went back to sleep until six.

He was either so lazy or malicious that whenever he wanted to know the time, he would ring for a servant—instead of turning his head to look at the clock. He refused to reach for a glass, whether of water or whiskey, but summoned a lackey to hand it to him.

He ate like a horse and exercised like a sloth. He grew so corpulent that his legs could not carry his weight; in time, a servant on either side had to hold him up as he toddled around a room. He was so obscene, even when sober, that to this day some of his letters have never been published. The Grand Duchess of Russia met George in 1814 and said: "His vaunted amiability really consists of the most licentious, dirty talk I ever heard in my life."

Thomas Lawrence's portrait of this royal cox-
comb captures the puffy vanity, the petulance,
the cute coiffure, the layers of gaudy raiment, the
whiskey-tinted nose, the rouged cheeks, the sen-
sual cupid lips. Read Thackeray's scorching vi-
gnette:

> His biographers say that when he commenced
> housekeeping in that splendid new palace
> (Brighton), the Prince of Wales had some
> windy projects (for) encouraging the arts. . . .
> Fiddle-sticks! French ballet-dancers, horse-
> jockeys, buffoons, procurers, tailors, boxers,
> fencing-masters, jewel and gimcrack mer-
> chants—these were his real companions. . . .
> dandies and parasites. . . . He was a creature of
> monstrous vanity, and levity incurable. . . . He
> was timid . . . heartless and treacherous . . . a
> worn-out voluptuary. . . .

Even this vituperation does not prepare one for
the story of George's amours, nor the fantastic
cast of characters who surrounded him.

Among the playmates (one was Beau Brummel)
who latched on to George Augustus Frederick in
his Xanadu was the Princesse de Lamballe. This
Parisian beauty fainted twice a week, regularly,
always at the same hour. She remained unconscious for precisely thirty minutes. Whenever the
Princesse was frightened, she emitted shrieks
akin to those of a panicky peacock. She would go
into a seizure over the damndest things: a nose-

gay of violets, the sight of a lobster, even a painting which contained a shellfish. The Princesse was
not Jewish; she was just neurotic.

She was so devoted to her royal mistress, Marie
Antoinette, that she left Brighton for Paris one
morning in 1791, bravely stayed by the Queen's
side, and was seized by the revolutionary mob—
who literally tore her to pieces. Her pretty head
they placed on a pike and marched to her hair-
dresser, commanding the poor *perruquier* to
rouge the cheeks and comb the hair in the long
style the Princesse had favored. Then the noble
children of *liberté* sped to the Tuileries and
taunted the royal family with the hideous trophy.
Refreshed by gloatings, the horde proceeded to
the Palais Royal and broke into the chambers of
the Duc d'Orléans. That chevalier was just about
to sit down to an *intime* repast with his mistress,
Agnes de Buffon, when Danton's progeny waved
the gruesome token before his eyes.

The Duc studied the piked head and sighed,
"Ah, my dear Agnes, it is the Princesse de Lamballe. I recognize her coiffure. Let us dine."

Another habitué of the Royal Pavilion was the
celebrated actress, Mrs. Mary Robinson, who
rode around Brighton in a scarlet phaeton, broke
many a heart, and slept in many bed. She was
known as "Perdita," from the role she played in
one of David Garrick's blithe versions of Shake-
speare. For a time she was the Prince's favorite.

Perdita was more than somewhat theatrical. Every day she changed her costume for a new *persona:* one day a soubrette, another a peasant, once a "cravetted Amazon of the horse." The versatile actress developed acute rheumatism, alas, but the affliction released unsuspected creative powers; Perdita wrote such engaging poems that she was hailed as England's Sappho. The hailing was excessive.

Another beauty in the set that buzzed around the Prince was Lady Lade. Once mistress of "Sixteen String Jack," a highwayman whom she saw hanged, Lady Lade was renowned for her lusty vocabulary. When the Prince of Wales danced with her at the Royal Pavilion, a covey of titled women huffed out of the ballroom.

One of the umbrageous was Elizabeth Luttrell. Her rectitude was spurious. She ran a faro table, was arrested for some shenanigan, and landed in gaol. But she bribed her way out and fled to Germany, where she proceeded to line her pockets by picking those of others. Apprehended in this ignoble art, the Lady was sentenced to clean the streets of Augsburg—whilst chained to a wheelbarrow. She had the good sense to terminate the humiliation by swallowing poison.

I must pile Ossa on Pelion. The Prince of Wales' impetuosity reached its true fulfillment in his passion for twice-widowed Maria Anna Fitzherbert.

He courted her all over Brighton and London, before scores of sympathetic observers, with the most exorbitant gestures and entreaties. But Mrs. Fitzherbert refused to be his mistress. She was Catholic.

So George Augustus Frederick was driven to the extremity of marrying her—secretly. (He would have forfeited his right to the throne had the marriage to a Catholic been made public.) Mrs. Fitzherbert had consulted the Vatican before agreeing to marry a Protestant—prince or no prince. The Holy See assured her that the nuptials would be valid, even if performed by an Anglican.

The wedding took place in the bride's home. A young minister sworn to secrecy administered the holy rites, for which he received £500 in cash and sundry promises of favor once George became king. Only the bride's uncle, her brother, and Orlando Bridgeman, a crony of the Prince, witnessed the ceremony. All kept mum.

The morganatic union was never known to the Prince's father, loopy King George III, who loathed his son. At a royal luncheon the monarch once seized his heir apparent by the throat, flung him against a wall, and proceeded to choke him. The Prince burst into tears. The King released him and sighed to his guests, "See how my sadness upsets him." This is a rare case of the pot calling the kettle white.

George III suffered periodic fits of insanity,

which turned into permanent lunacy (it is now known he was a victim of a blood disease), whereupon the Prince of Wales became Regent. But his powers were strictly limited, so disliked was he by both Parliament and people for his notorious dissipations and monumental debts.

Now, the Prince had never admitted his marriage to Mrs. Fitzherbert; and she was too loyal to confirm the alliance. Mrs. Fitzherbert was not allowed to appear at court in London, though the Queen, the Prince's mother, openly received Lady Jersey, the Prince's new (or renewed) paramour, who was Protestant. So the clandestine approval of the Vatican was trumped by the public prejudice of Whitehall. I, for one, am pleased that George Augustus Frederick himself showed not the slightest sign of intolerance when in heat. He often reviled his loved ones ("infernal Jezebel," "depraved harlot"), but his words did not diminish his lust.

Rumors about the secret marriage to Mrs. Fitzherbert so agitated London that the Prince Regent asked Charles James Fox to squelch them. Fox knew nothing of the nuptials. That superb orator rose in the House of Commons to make a thunderous speech labeling all the allegations a "miserable calumny." That night, Fox ran into Orlando Bridgeman, who said, "You have been misinformed, sir. I was present at the marriage."

I do not know what Fox replied. I do know he died not long after.

In 1795, drowning in debt, the Prince asked Parliament to bail him out. The Lords set one condition: that he marry a cousin, Princess Caroline of Brunswick-Wolfenbüttel. George sent Lord Malmesbury to fetch his bride-to-be from Germany. (Bigamy never troubled his thoughts.) When she was ushered into the Prince's presence, he turned pale, broke into a sweat, and cried, "I am not well. Brandy!"

I cannot blame him. Caroline of Brunswick-Wolfenbüttel was dumpy, silly, unbelievably vulgar—and she smelled. She had a pathological aversion to water. She never washed, they said, and rarely changed her underthings. She was oversexed as well as overweight, ready to diddle with any stud within the royal circle or the royal stables. She cackled as she flirted, and giggled as she ogled. She was, in short, a travesty of a princess, whose "manners were of the farmyard and the taproom." She had all the charm of a Wolfenbüttel.

The Prince of Wales got himself stone drunk and "looked like a corpse" when, on April 8, 1795, he married Caroline. During the entire ceremony he remained comatose, but Caroline chortled triumphantly.

The Prince was so revolted by his bride that he performed his conjugal duty on the wedding night—once, and never again. (The hateful encounter produced a daughter, Princess Charlotte.) Three days later, George Augustus Frederick made a will, in his own hand, bequeathing everything he owned to "my wife, the wife of my heart and soul"—Mrs. Fitzherbert. The will stayed secret; so did the bigamy.

The Prince and Princess moved into Carlton House in London, but her presence filled him with such nausea that he fled her proximity and refused to speak to her. Instead he wrote her letters—which she was obliged to answer. The correspondence sped back and forth across the shortest postal zone in English history: all indoors.

Soon after his disastrous marriage to Caroline, George wrote her a beautifully phrased ukase (she was not more than two hundred feet away):

> Let our intercourse be restricted to tranquil and comfortable society. . . . I shall not infringe the terms of the restriction by proposing, at any period, a connexion of a more particular nature. I shall now close this disagreeable correspondence. . . .

"A connexion of a more particular nature" must rank among the finest euphemisms of our tongue.

Between the Prince of Wales' visible loathing, the Princess' promiscuity, and the gossip of the servant platoons in Carlton House, the nonconnubiality of the royal pair was soon known all over London. Any who doubted the facts were converted to the truth when the Prince boldly appointed a mistress, Lady Jersey, Lady-in-Waiting to his consort. Indeed, Caroline appeared in public with increased zest, affecting the sorrow of a maiden betrayed; those who detested the Prince showered her with sympathy.

Throughout these tangled days, Mrs. Fitzherbert made no waves. She was silent, cool, and—I suspect—confident that in the end true love would triumph.

George lost interest in Lady Jersey, as those who knew him were not surprised to learn, and pined for Mrs. Fitzherbert again. He begged her to come back to his arms, which was easy, and his bed, which was not. But she did—after receiving the renewed approval of the Pope. His Holiness declared the Prince's union with Princess Caroline null and void; after all, Mrs. Fitzherbert had married him before.

And now, whenever the Prince and Mrs. Fitzherbert (it was still not known they were married) appeared together in a royal box, at Covent Garden or a theater, Princess Caroline attended as well, flaunting her betrayal with unseemly glee.

In 1814, to George's relief, Princess Caroline left England for Italy, palpitating in estrus. A four-flushing Lothario named Pergami soon serviced her and wrapped new scandal around her name. Once a phaeton of gold and mother-of-pearl, shaped like a seashell, carried England's Princess of Wales through Genoa—preceded by her lover on a white horse, dressed (for some reason) as General Murat. Caroline, who was not at ease with discretion, sprawled conspicuously in the back seat, waving to one and all, a fat doll in pink feathers and a short skirt pulled above her knees, which advertised her sausage legs—in high boots.

Caroline caused so much brouhaha on the Continent that after she returned to England, her husband, now George IV, arranged to have her hauled into the House of Lords; he was hell-bent on getting a bill of divorce. The hearings made quite a spectacle in that magnificent chamber. The evidence of Caroline's hanky-panky was lurid and copious, but not quite enough to impress some sympathetic Lords and an indignant populace. The action for divorce was "withdrawn." George IV was outraged by the disloyalty of his peers.

The exuberant Caroline arrived at Westminster Abbey for her husband's coronation—and her own. She came in full regalia, ready to be anointed. But she was not allowed to enter the cathedral. Many English folk criticized George for such a public humiliation; others wondered why he had not strangled her in private. He was saved from further anguish when, a year later, Caroline departed this raunchy vale.

George had lived with Mrs. Fitzherbert for nine love-locked years, had cast her aside, had resumed their cohabitation for six years more, had abandoned her again—and never admitted he had married her. (They had one child, a son, who went to America.) What sort of man *was* this?

George Rex ; he went to
South Africa !

Despite Thackeray, or my animadversions, he was not a fool. Spoiled, intemperate, dissolute, to be sure, but not an idiot. He was, in fact, clever and quite witty. He spoke excellent French, German, Italian. He was a connoisseur of painting (he started the great collection of the National Gallery) and a sensitive judge of literature. He recognized the talent of Walter Scott, whom he knighted; and, considerably ahead of the mandarins of literature, acclaimed the genius of Jane Austen. He collected the superb French furniture which today adorns Buckingham Palace. His taste in architecture may be seen in the curving beauty of Regent Street (named in his honor), the majestic mansions and colonnades which Nash designed around Regent's Park.

George wrote in a style that compels my admiration. You may find it pompous, but you must remember the orotundities of prose which were fashionable in those days. To his daughter Charlotte, George once addressed this confused but impressive *cri de coeur:*

> You have no reason to apprehend a union with the Prince of Orange, the grievous calamity which I, alas!, my dearest child, have experienced from a marriage with a person whose character we have had occasion so recently, so fully and so freely to gather, and from the contemplation of which it is so much my wish to abstain. (You know) the wicked art and depraved contrivances of your mother.... We can-

not marry like the rest of the world, for both
our elevated rank and our religious faith limit
our choice to few indeed.

The Duke of Wellington, an eminently sober
figure, favored with George IV's trust and affection, wrote:

> He was indeed the most extraordinary com-
> pound of talent, wit, buffoonery, obstinancy,
> and good feeling—in short, a medley of the
> most opposite qualities, with a great prepon-
> derance of good—that I ever saw in any char-
> acter in my life.

Thackeray later inveighed against

> a pantomime king with a pantomime wife and
> pantomime courtiers whom he pokes with his
> pantomime sceptre. . . . It is monstrous, gro-
> tesque, laughable, with its prodigious little-
> ness, etiquettes, ceremonials, sham moralities
> . . . as absurd and outrageous as Punch's pup-
> pet show. . . . There is no stronger satire on the
> proud English society of that day, than that
> they admired George.

I certainly do not admire George. But I adore
his Royal Pavilion.

Just before this mountainous victim of gluttony
and concupiscence expired, in his sixty-eighth
year, he asked, in pain and fever, for Mrs. Fitzher-

bert. She was the only woman, I think, he had ever truly loved—for long. After George IV breathed his last, they found a locket under his nightshirt: it contained her portrait.

They also found in his bedchamber the damndest hodgepodge of "treasures" which he had hoarded for half a century: old pantaloons, frayed capes, ladies' gloves and garters, locks of hair from one-night lovers, yellowed letters, dried-out flowers—and five hundred purses, his own purses, each one stuffed with money. The cache came to £10,000.

I close reluctantly, with a passage from Clifford Musgrave's *Royal Pavilion:*

> George IV . . . did not explore the melancholy aspects of romanticism. . . . For his fantasies of Chinese gaiety or splendour, or of Indian Mogul magnificence, were all in a key of pleasure and delight, a world where the mind disported itself forever in fancy dress. . . .
>
> Today almost all the paradisal lands of the imagination are vanished. But the Pavilion may still remind us (of) the vision of a golden age . . . an experiment in dazzling splendour that made another attempt inconceivable.

I ask you: Is it not worth a sixty-minute ride from London to gaze upon the inconceivable?

☐   ☐

GENEVA:
The Social Whirl

From the terrace of the villa, we gazed down, down upon the moonlit mirror of the lake. Centuries of no history stretched around us. Charles, my old friend and host, now delegated to some international moribundity, and his wife and I contemplated the supernal scene.

Suddenly Charles trilled: "Ah, beautiful, *beautiful* Switzerland! . . . See the noble Alps, the peaceful meadows. . . . Is any place on earth so sweet to behold, so soothing to the soul? . . . I tell you, Maggie, all this serenity is making me a goddamn nervous wreck!"

His wife moaned. "The Casino! How about some gambling, dear?"

Charles made gargling noises.

"Why not?" I chimed in cheerily. "I love casinos."

He eyed me nastily. "All right, laughing boy. Let's live it up."

Maggie drove the Peugeot down the luminous, lyrical landscape. I felt as if we were falling off the edge of a postcard.

The Casino was not what the word suggests. It was dreary, a bumpkin cousin to the ornate parlors dedicated to roulette and *chemin de fer* which I had admired in Monte Carlo or a clandestine clip joint on Sunset Boulevard.

Geneva's temple of fortune was as quiet as a hospital waiting room. It contained precisely nine glum gamblers, all Swiss: stocky, ruddy, visibly hygienic. The men wore stiff-shouldered jackets:

the ladies flaunted devil-may-care dirndls which were all the rage around the time William Tell took aim at the apple.

Charles chortled over my dismay, then directed my attention to a sign I still have difficulty believing. It was a large, neat placard, hung from the ceiling, and proclaimed the house rules with faultless clarity in three languages:

NOTICE
MINIMUM BET: ONE FRANC
MAXIMUM BET: TWO FRANCS

After an audacious half-hour at the roulette table, during which Maggie won six francs and I lost four (Charles just sat at the bar, grinning at us), we translated our silent consensus into action and trudged back to the car.

During the sylvan ascent to the villa, no one said a word. We were too busy hating—the Casino, the lake, the moonlight, the Alps.

□   □

VALHALLA ON SECOND AVENUE

I saw my first play in an inelegant theater on Blue Island Avenue in Chicago. It was a Yiddish play. The production—all actors, sets, costumes—came to us on royal tour from New York. So great a gift from Nineveh was a considerable event in Chicago. An "Original New York Production" offered us fabled stars: beautiful Bertha Kalish, homeric Boris Thomashevsky, matchless Jacob Adler, Maurice Schwartz, Jacob ben-Ami.

I was seven years old, and my parents, who adored the theater, took me to a Sunday matinée "benefit." The Jewish stage depended for its very life on "benefits"—that is, underwritings of a play by a union or fraternal lodge, a *bund* of immigrants from the same hometown in Europe, or the Workmen's Circle. . . . Any performance "SOLD OUT!" was a tried and true "benefit."

I saw half a dozen Yiddish repertory companies before my manhood, from the great People's Theater to the immortal Habima, the Yiddish Art Theater and glamorous companies from Warsaw and Moscow. In later years, whenever I visited New York I would hasten to the temples of drama on Second Avenue. After the theater, it was *de rigueur* to go to the Café Royal (pronounced Royál), *alav-ha-sholem.*

The "Royal," at Twelfth Street and Second Avenue, was the Sardi's and Lindy's and "21" of the Jewish intelligentsia: famous writers, editors, critics, composers, poets and, of course, the stars of the Yiddish stage who drew swarms of idol-

atrous fans. Devotees were as fervent in their loyalty to the Royal as Irish writers were to Costello's
Bar, or *The New Yorker's* staff to the Algonquin.

Sometimes the Royal was called the "Ki-
bitzarnia," a nickname both affectionate and ironic
for the nightly audience of *kibitzers:* i.e., self-ap-
pointed experts, advisers and quidnuncs. (*Kibitzer*
comes from the German name for a peewit, a bird
never seen on the Lower East Side, renowned for
its inquisitive twitterings.)

The Café Royal featured Hungarian cuisine
(chicken *paprikash,* goulash, heavenly *palatschin-
ken*), but its hypnotic power emanated from its
clientele. As one Royalite told me: "Averybody
who's *eny*body" in the creative cauldrons of the
Lower East Side turned up at the restaurant at *least*
one night a week. To dine there was a public
demonstration of Culture; to eavesdrop there was
manna to the soul; to be seen there was a *sine
qua non* of status.

The "in" night at the Royal was Friday. Atten-
dance on Saturdays was prestigious; Mondays
were plebeian: but Friday nights were obligatory
for the *crème de la crème.* For every Friday, the
pages of the *Forward* or *Freiheit* or *Der Tag* bulged
with dramatic criticism, political *feuilletons,* re-
views of a novel by Sholem Asch or the stories of
I. J. Singer (Isaac Bashevis' older brother), or the
latest tale by the "Mark Twain of Yiddish literature," Sholem Aleichem.

Thunderous editorials provoked fierce letters

from readers: on the state of *Yiddishkeit,* the stratagems of trade unions, the laudable or insidious trend of Assimilation, the crises confronting the Working Class Movement. Partisan columnists waved the banners of choleric factions: pious Zionists denouncing secular Socialists, Bundists battling Communists, champions of Hebrew castigating propagandists for Yiddish, spokesmen for "the People" flaying the Left for preaching revolution or Social Democrats for defending the ballot of perfidious Capitalism.

I doubt whether the coffeehouses of Vienna or Budapest rang with such passionate debates as one could hear in the all-night cafeterias strung along Delancey Street or Houston, or—in its final, brilliant, doomed stand—in the peerless Café Royal.

✡✡✡

I first went to the Royal on a Friday night before the crowds arrived, to talk to the waiters as they ate their own dinners. It was with pride ("Am I talking for publication?") that they recounted tales about the celebrities they had served: Georgie Jessel ("a boy from around here hisself"), Ed Sullivan ("his wife's Jewish"), Paul Muni ("You know he was a child actor *in this neighborhood,* real name Muni Weisenfreund"), Leonard Lyons ("a doll"), two of the Marx Brothers, George Burns, Smith and Dale ("You could bust your *sides* laughing on 'Doctor Krankheit!' ").

One waiter vouchsafed, "Name me a name, a name it has *talent,* and I give you ten-to-one they been here in the Royal!" Another characterized his clientele according to the food they favored: "Alfred Lunt? Goulash. . . . Jack Benny? Wiener schnitzel. . . . Will Durant, you heard of him, a real philosopher, gentile? Cheesecake."

The waiters felt that the Royal was a quasi-public institution, a sanctuary for artists in a philistine world. "Actors are practically *living* here!" one exclaimed.

"The Royal is like their home."

"No Café Royal, no culture!"

"Culture for the *messes!*"

"Messes-shmesses, culture is univoisal!"

The captain of the corps rose. "Time."

As his crew snuffed out cigarettes, tilted tea glasses dry, donned white jackets for the evening ahead, the headwaiter took me aside: *"Boychik,* talk to the Stars, when they start coming in, and you'll hear enough for a book. A book as fat as the telephone dictionary!"

The Royal followed the European practice of holding waiters financially responsible for the provender they served. Any waiter whom a patron could persuade to put the bill "on the cuff" would pay the tab out of his own pocket. The Royal was rife with persuaders.

The most celebrated subsidizer of artists hard-pressed for cash was "Herman," who appeared in

Broadway's gossip columns as "The Millionaire Busboy." He was at a table near the back, among the pinochle and *klabiotsh* players for whom the Royal had set aside a special *plotz*. Herman was resting his arches and soothing his gullet with a sardine-and-cream-cheese sandwich, garnished with slices of onion. I introduced myself.

"Call me Hoiman," he said. "You want introview me?"

I shielded my surprise. "Yes."

"So siddon—an' esk."

Within two minutes I realized that Herman was a master interviewee. Drawing him out was a cinch; in fact, whenever my drawing-out powers flagged, he drew himself out. "Why you don't esk how long I *am*?" he blurted at one point.

"How long are you?"

"Here tvunty-nine yiss! Write don. Same place. Same jop. Naxt?"

Herman's pate was bald, his face round, and rarely have I gazed into so vacuous a deadpan. The closest Herman came to communicating a shred of emotion was when he blinked. He blinked blankly, but he blinked.

I had heard that Herman's wealth derived from his cashing of checks for patrons. The Royal refused to honor checks—anyone's checks; the management simply did not *believe* in checks. Herman did. To test his mettle, I asked, "Would you cash a personal check of mine?"

"Homoch?"

"Ten dollars."

Herman lifted himself out of his chair and studied my shoes.

"Do you judge people by—their *shoes?*" I gulped.

"Soitinly. Poor man, poor shoe. Rich man, expansive shoe."

"How much will you charge me?"

Herman screwed up one dolorous eye. "Tan dollar? Cost you saventy-tri sants."

I thought this usurious, considering my honest features. "How do you arrive at that?"

"Pretsent," he shrugged. He made no effort to explain what the percent was.

I bade him adieu.

A friend came in and I ordered coffee for two. He initiated me into some choice examples of Yiddish-theater argot: A *nukhshlepper* is a hanger-on to one of fame; a *fiermacher* ("firemaker") a ham whose *shtick* can burn even an asbestos curtain into protest; a *bulbenik* an actor who muffs or massacres his lines. "See that table? The man alone? Dipping the sugar cube in his tea? . . . He is the King of the *Bulbeniks!* A sad case. He works two–three weeks, then makes such a *bulbe* he won't get another part for a year. . . . Some *mishegoss* in his head makes him commit such crazy boo-boos you could die!"

"What do you mean?"

"Well, on the stage, sooner or later, he has to say what he sees." My friend meditated. "I'll give you an example. In one play, the *Bulbenik* came front center, held out his hands in tragic appeal, and—all through rehearsals—delivered this beautiful line: 'Oh, dear God, I have five children—five dear, sweet *kinder*. . . .' But on opening night, the *Bulbenik* comes front center, puts out his hands and says, 'Oh dear God, I have five finger—five dear, sweet finger. . . .' What a *scandall!* What a disaster . . .

"I'll give you another 'for instance.' In *The Dybbuk*, you will remember that the maiden, all in white, is possessed by a demon, a *dybbuk*. She writhes, she cries out in terror, she faints—and falls to the floor. The maiden lays there in the spotlight, alone, unconscious. . . . Now a group of villagers enter, each one holding a candle. They see the maiden's lifeless form. They draw back in horror. Their leader steps closer and cries, 'A *dybbuk!* A *dybbuk* has entered the maiden!' Cries, screams, such a *tummel* of fear sweeps the villagers! A powerful scene—right?—never surpassed. . . . So, came opening night. The maiden is in the clutches of the evil spirit. She writhes and cries and fights the invisible *dybbuk*. She weakens, she faints, she collapses. . . . The villagers appear. They see the touching, lifeless form. They draw back in terror. Their leader steps forward, slowly, raises his candle to see better—

and cries, 'A candle! A candle has entered the maiden!' " My friend shook his head in woe. "That was the *Bulbenik.*"

I pitied the forlorn figure sitting alone at a distant table, sucking on his tea-soaked cube of sugar, shunned by all who knew his awful propensity.

"Second Avenue" produced the classics of the Western world: *King Lear, Faust, The Cherry Orchard*—all performed in Yiddish with a grandeur of mood and feats of acting that matched London or old Budapest or Berlin. But New York's immigrant audiences particularly loved those classics which were "adapted"—and how they were adapted!

Take *Hamlet.* On Second Avenue the locale was changed from Denmark to a village in Poland. Hamlet's noble father was changed from a king to a rabbi. Hamlet's dastardly uncle did not usurp the throne by administering poison to Hamlet's beloved father. Oh, no. He gave the old rabbi a fatal heart attack by seducing Hamlet's mother— while Hamlet was away from home, studying at some *yeshiva* on his road to the rabbinate. Rosencrantz and Guildenstern were obviously Jews, disgusting backstabbers and *paskudnyaks.* Polonius was assumed, I assume, to have changed his name from Polonsky. And after sweet Ophelia's death, Hamlet held heartrending vigil in the graveyard—where he married his dead love, in a ceremony sanctioned by orthodox tradition.

Or take *A Doll's House*. It was renamed *Minna* and transferred from Norway to New York. In its Yiddish manifestation, Ibsen's classic recounted the tragedy of a Jewish mother and daughter smitten, separately and simultaneously, with The Boarder. What transpired between The Boarder, his landlady and her daughter (Minna's father was a lout) must have made Ibsen moan in his grave, but it was a smash at the box office.

New plays were written in Yiddish, for the young Jewish stage, by I. L. Peretz, Jacob Gordin, Peretz Hirshbein. Ansky's immortal *Dybbuk* or I. J. Singer's poignant *Yoshe Kalb* were as powerful and memorable as the best of Broadway or Drury Lane. As the Yiddish theater prospered, a new and immensely popular type of play appeared. Their very names describe their attraction: *The Cousin from Odessa, A Mother's Tears, The Rag-Picker from Minsk, A Sewing Girl's Plight*. . . . These juicy stories dealt with the clash between Orthodox fathers and Socialist sons; the traditions of the *shtetl* besieged by the Sodom of America; guilt about money, earned with sweat and begged for in letters from the Old Country, where parents and grandparents aged and waited and might never be seen again; a Jewish boy in love with a *shiksa* or (less often) a Jewish girl bewitched by a *goy;* the throat-filling *Kaddish* for the dead and

the joyous Bar Mitzvah woven into the eternal tri-
angle of Amour; defections from the synagogue—
or the union; faithful wives crushed by faithless
husbands, pious fathers slapping "fancy" daugh-
ters, the plight of "greenhorns," the venality of
Bosses. . . .

Purist critics scourged these melodramas as
"onion plays," deploring the easy tears to which
they pandered. It was in vain.

The final fare for a dying "Second Avenue" was
unashamedly commercial: plays which spiced Jewish themes with American vaudeville, introduced
burlesque to drag laughs in by the heel, stooped
to broad characters and "street talk" as vivid as
it was vulgar. The stories were steeped in un-
deniable *shlock*. The critics cursed and the classi-
cists railed against such *chazzerai* ("garbage"). The
Yiddish press flayed producers and playwrights
and players for desecrating the sacred Theater
(a forum, a schoolroom, a temple to edify the
masses) with such disgusting *shmattas* ("rags"). . . .
But when has *ars gratia artis* prevailed against
"How many standees tonight?"

Whatever the plays, whether noble or base, to
Lower East Side audiences the Stage was a dream
world, a vision of opulence and romance. Anyone
who actually performed on the *bema* was touched
with aristocracy. Even supporting players were
doused with admiration. Stars were lionized.
When great Jacob Adler returned to the stage,
after a widely mourned malady, the billboards

proclaimed: "The splendid eagle will spread his wings again!"

✢✢✢

One night I went to the Royal with an actor who was a denizen of the premises. I noticed a large, round Western Union clock on a side wall. At a table under the clock sat a sour, dour man. Opposite him a pretty soubrette was importuning him with vivid gestures. Behind her, perhaps fifteen people queued.

"That *farbissener* under the clock is the manager of the Actors' Union," said my friend. "The lineup are actors who want a job, or at least an audition. The union *k'nocker* interviews them . . ."

"*Here?*"

"Where else?"

"Why not his office?"

"This is better than his office. His office is a cuckoo house. Also, it closes."

At this moment, a waiter, holding the receiver of a wallphone, sang out, "Long distance!"

The *k'nocker* promptly left his table to take the call.

"That could be a producer in the Catskills calling," said my friend, "or a director from Cleveland, St. Louis, Asbury Park."

I learned that "under the clock" was the brain for a theatrical nervous system which stretched from Far Rockaway to Los Angeles. A road company stranded in Milwaukee (the promoter had absconded with the "take"); a director needing a replacement in Omaha (the leading lady had lost her voice); an impresario in Chicago enraged by actors' quarrels about billing; a spokesman for a troupe in Philadelphia ready to call a strike— anyone bedeviled by such crises far from home would call "under the clock."

To the *k'nocker* "under the clock" directors and producers poured out their needs in person. Who's available for Desdemona's maid in *Othello from Odessa?* Who can play the "singlemon" in *A Broken Heart?* How much will the union ask for nonspeaking parts in *Crime and Punishment?* Is young Kaminsky "at liberty"? How reach that scene chewer from *The Goldeneh Medina?* . . . So wide was the knowledge, and so various the power, of the *k'nocker.*

The crowd began to enter the Royal, and the decibels mounted. Talk—liquid, heated, intricate talk in Yiddish, English, Yinglish, Polish, Russian, Romanian—blared all around me. A composer (he wore a velvet ascot) crooned a song to three admiring ladies. Several actresses discussed the cadence of a passage. A poet (he wore a beret) declaimed an ode to a prospective Medici. Coffee cups clattered. Tea glasses tinkled. Rockets of laughter punctured the air.

From every side now, waiters yelled, men argued, women protested. Two actors rehearsed some dialogue from Gogol. Someone burst into

Hebrew (from Bialik?) with rapture. . . . The fat, fecund sounds twisted themselves into the echoing of a great seashell. I felt lonely.

My friend named the plays from which both cast and audience were streaming into the café. "But wait. Soon the real Stars will arrive!"

A stormy argument caught my ear. "That play is—plain and simple—*chazzerai!*"

"So why did a man like Maurice Schwartz pick it?"

"He's an *artist*," a woman snapped, "so he's stubborn."

"A *mule* is stubborn, also."

"How can you tell the difference?"

"A mule isn't a Maurice Schwartz!"

"Ha, ha, ha, I'll *bust* laughing, I should live so."

Another exchange held me spellbound. "The story stinks!"

" 'Stinks'! Why *stinks,* all of a sutton? It's foist-class directed, no?"

"No."

"You are some *mavin.*"

"I am some honest!"

"*Puleez,* Veintraub. Believe it to me, you're a hard man to satisfy."

Around 11:20, expectancy swept the tables. The Stars were arriving. Their Entrances were worthy of Versailles. They hesitated in the doorway just long enough to be recognized, applauded, acclaimed: profiles tilted, eyes world-weary, the brave smile an exhausted artist owes his courtiers, the wan sigh of players still lost in their role. . . .

The Actresses wore spangled capes and cascading hats, the Actors greatcoats with caracul collars. Long scarves were tossed across brave shoulders. White gloves were clasped in limp hands. As the procession from Parnassus came through those lucky doors, the enraptured Royalties heralded each star by name, adding "Oh!"s and "Ah!"s and "Look! Look!"s. Some fans just burst into applause.

As the Children of Make-Believe strolled through the tables, they affected the humility expected by their admirers: "You really enjoyed my performance?" Some malingered with éclat: "I had such a headache tonight—a migraine like hot needles—it's a miracle I remembered my lines!" Some wallowed in vanity: "Such applause! You stayed past the final curtain? You ever *heard* such clapping? Such 'Bravos'? An absolute ovation!"

Two conversations still caress my ears:

RIPENED ACTRESS
The truth, Avrum, I beg of you—the truth! How was I?

LOYAL FRIEND
You were marvelous! Magnificent!

ACTRESS
You mean that?

LOYAL FRIEND
On my mother's grave, I swear it!

ACTRESS
(sighing)
Thank you, Avrum. If only our *volk,* our audiences, had more people like you. . . . Oh,
Avrum, Avrum, I pour out each night my life's
blood.

The second colloquy:

ACTOR
Tired . . . ? Yes, Mirele, I am tired. . . . A *mon*ster,
the producer. The director, a *man*iac. . . . How did
you like my performance?

MIRIAM
*Gen*ius! Tonight you touch *genius!*

ACTOR
(with a *moué*)
Tonight I wasn't exactly genius, Mirele. *Wednesday* you should of seen me. *Wednesday* I was a
genius.

The Great Ones permitted the maître d' to lead
them to conspicuous tables, where ensued a
flurry of huggings, kissings, cheek touchings;
hand pattings and arm squeezings; flamboyant
phrasings of praise, impulsive expressions of adu-

lation. I doubt whether there have been such rustlings and bustlings since the Congress of Vienna.

"Observe there," crowed my friend. "There" was a prized corner table, near the entrance, where an imposing, mascaraed dowager, perhaps seventy, held court. Votaries crowded around her chair, hanging on to her every word; behind them, acolytes bent their heads and cupped their ears. The lady's monologue elicited murmuring "Mm-mm!"s and marveling *"Mnyeh!"s,* chortles of assent and sonatas of delight. *"That* is Mrs. Adler."

I felt fortunate to see Sarah Adler, wife of Jacob Adler, with whom she had often costarred. The First Lady of Second Avenue was, besides, mother of Luther and Stella Adler, both of whom had gone on to stardom in the Group Theater and Hollywood.

Mrs. Adler's talent was mighty, her aplomb renowned, her life-style startling. She rarely went to bed before 4 A.M.; she never rose before noon. She was believed to be indestructible. Indeed, one story describes a group of tourists in the year 2000 being shown through the Royal. "At that table," the guide declaims, "sat the great Thomashevsky. . . . There sat Jennie Goldstein, idol of soap operas. . . . And that corner table was always reserved for—oh, hel*lo,* Mrs. Adler!"

Once a young reporter asked this extraordinary lady, "There are so many rumors about your true age, Mrs. Adler . . ."

"I am forty-two."

"Forty-two?" echoed the journalist. "But Mrs. Adler, I just talked to your daughter Stella, and she told me that she is thirty-one!"

"Stella," the *grande-dame* murmured, "lives her life; I lead mine."

Jacob Adler, a considerable Don Juan, was once on tour when a woman he had romanced years earlier came backstage after one of his performances, leading a handsome boy. "Jacob, darling, this is your son!"

Adler surveyed the alleged product of his loins. "A fine young man. Here, my boy—" and he handed the youth two free passes to the show.

The lady exclaimed, "Jacob! We are very poor. We need *bread!*"

Replied Adler, "I am an actor, madame. From me you get passes; for bread, sleep with a baker."

At 3 A.M., the Royal lights dimmed, brightened, dimmed. . . . The card players in the back began to settle up. Some of the restaurant forum rose with reluctance.

My friend said, "Don't rush. We've got another *hour.*"

But I was too drained of emotion to stay on. The tables I passed on my way out reverberated with partisan ardors:

1.

"Him you call a composer?"

"Him I call another Oiving Berlin!"

"Him tell, 'You should write music for the deaf!' "

2.

An overwrought lady: "Talent he has? Maybe. *Brains* he has? Never!"

"Who said actors need *brains?*" demanded her adversary.

"They couldn't *hurt.*"

3.

"Minsky? *Feh!* He is a shame to our people!"

"He only gives the public what they want. . . . "

"That type public are dumbbells, *prost,* vulgar—"

"So that's the type public made Minsky a monte-millionaire!"

"Who can argue with you?!"

"Don't argue with *me;* go argue with Success!"

As I left the incomparable chamber, those voices—undaunted, undiminished—still sang behind me.

☨☨☨

Postscript:

Yiddish is a dying tongue. The grandchildren of the immigrants from Eastern Europe barely understand it—if they understand it at all. So today, in a frantic effort to tie American progeny to their past, the Yiddish stage uses contemporary plots and a bastard tongue in which English (for the young) and Yiddish (for their elders) alternate in startling phrasings.

The last play I saw on the Lower East Side was a "Comedy with Music" featuring that ageless, gifted gamin, Molly Picon. The story involved an old *zayde* ("grandfather") who lived with his daughter and son-in-law in an affluent suburb of New York. The *zayde* tried very hard to bridge the abyss which separated him from his beloved grandson, "Bruce." The very notion of a Jewish lad named Bruce is eye-popping; besides, the *zayde* called his grandson "Bruceleh."

I shall never forget the climactic moment when Bruceleh's mother, discovering that her husband had been conducting hanky-panky with a blonde neighbor of generous girth and morals, cried: *"Und hawst du gedenkt as Ich ken leben* in the shadow of another woman?!" ("And did you think I can live in the shadow of another woman?!")

Young and old alike, in that audience, gasped.

SANTORINI: The Top of the World

A white mirage shimmered high up in the sky, shining clearer as the S.S. *Delos* skimmed across the Aegean. We sailed over a volcano, toward that iridescence ahead, far above us, something sparkling in the sunlight a thousand feet atop sheer perpendicularity. We glided past a low islet of cinders on our left: the charred peak of a mountain underneath the water.

In the tremendous eruption of 1500 B.C., the now-sunken volcano had exploded, its fire and convulsions covering the land beneath us in boiling pumice two hundred feet deep. The cone of the volcano had dropped inward, the whole crater collapsing, and the sea foamed in to fill the flaming cavity. An earthquake followed, so violent that a tidal wave swept sixty-five miles south to Crete, obliterating the Minoans, their temples and palaces and brilliant civilization in minutes. . . .

We drifted toward a dark lagoon from which the cliff ahead soared straight up—up, up—and the white images on top took shape: a spire, a dome, flat roofs, the huddled cluster of an impossible village. The ancient Greeks called this rock isle Thera; later men called it Santorin; the Italians named it Santorini, which is a corruption of "Saint Irene," this most southerly of the Sporades, or "scattered isles."

The palisade ahead was banded in odd, muted colors, for the porous rock of Santorini is striated: blue-black, pale purple, burned-out green. The village in the sky seemed to have no connection with the quay so far below.

We entered the shadowed bay and anchored in a blue lagoon. Boats carried us from the ship to a planked jetty. We had to crane our necks now to confirm the existence of the tiny white village crowning the unbelievable precipice.

The boatmen herded us into a very narrow *cul de sac,* and up some stone steps. The moment I reached the top step, a donkey materialized *below* me, and I was thrust down on the saddle. An attendant slapped the beast, which started bobbing up a steep, cobbled path, made a sharp 10 degree turn, lumbered further up the scary incline, then reversed direction in a hairpin turn, ascending in this way a succession of zigzags that seemed interminable.

From my saddle I saw the *Delos* receding below me until it seemed a toy boat in an immense bathtub. I looked up: the cliff was a dizzying maze of sharp turns. I remembered our guide on the ship had mumbled something about "over eight hundred steps for those who may—" (a sigh) "—choose to walk."

I felt giddy, yet exhilarated by a challenge that left me no choice but bravery. My donkey bobbed upward, upward, as I made my peace with God. The cliff below, the lagoon, the whole vast surface of the world itself fell away. I thought I was looking through the wrong end of a telescope.

At last, the final hairpin turn appeared. My donkey clopped around it. The globe of the earth swiveled before my eyes.

Something rubbed beneath my stirrup, and natives wafted me up and out of the saddle, onto the salvation of solid stone.

I stood up at last, weaving slightly, marveling over the curving, sweeping arc of the horizon. The whitewashed village of Thera lay around and below me, dazzling, snug, a Klee of domes, towers and jumbled houses. And as I turned my head to encompass the immense plate of the sea-world from the most majestic and unique perch on which I had ever stood, I saw—Donald Duck.

He was no hallucination. He was yapping at me from a large playbill pasted on the wall of a tobacconist's. The poster advertised the only movie theater on Santorini; but it was the eyes and bellicose beak and jaunty sailor hat of Donald Duck which dominated the placard, here in pristine, gleaming Thera atop that wonder of Vulcan's forge known as Santorini.

I took a picture of the playbill and mailed it, from Athens, to Walt Disney with this note:

> Dear Walt:
> Do you know what they call this squawking fowl in Greek? Donald Pa'pia. He's gazing at the sea from a peak higher than Darien.
>
> > Love,
> > Leo

Months later, in New York, Walt, unannounced, poked his head through the doorway of my office at *Look*. "That Greek duck was just dandy!" He grinned. "But the only Darien I know is in Connecticut."

A FAREWELL
TO ROME

One night on the Via Veneto, under a pretty café awning and gilded sconces out of the Gay Nineties, I sipped my cappuccino, slouched in a chair, and lazily watched the peacock parade: tourists and starlets and tarts; fortune hunters, movie anglers, breathtaking girls; the *nouveaux riches* with their long cigars and diamond-ringed pinkies, pasta-fattened wives and streamlined mistresses. Lined up before the Hotel Excelsior was the night legion of gigolos, signaling their availability to American divorcées and South American widows and lonely rich ladies yearning for romance or, at least, an escort for dinner and a cabaret.

Civil Guards strolled through the hubbub, always in pairs, sporting their cockade hats and silver scabbards. And amongst the jazzy intimations of the dissolute, occasional countryfolk in holiday clothes goggled over this scandalous new world.

My mind drifted across the sea of history as I wondered what I could possibly write about Rome that has not been written a thousand times before. Where to begin?

Surely not here, in the heart of *la dolce vita*, where the mood is brazen, the spirit cynical, the very air corrupted with the mindless vanity of purchased or promiscuous amour. There's not the slightest resemblance between these strutting parvenus and the Romans who built history's greatest empire.

Today's Italians want pleasure, not power; cars,

not colonies (thank God). They yearn to be rich, virile, above all, envied. For three decades, since World War II, Italian movies have shown us, with marvelous wit and irony, facets of a culture drunk with new-found affluence, possessed by the pursuit of whatever sates the senses.

"You know, no people enjoys debunking itself the way we Italians do," said my companion, Luigi Barzini, that patrician stoic. "We love to deplore our immorality."

This only deepens Rome's cynicism, enlisting honesty to forgive self-indulgence.

"Italy is 99 percent Catholic," said Barzini, "so, the saying goes, our men repent each Sunday for what they did on Saturday and will repeat on Monday. It's also hard to play poker when you lay down three kings and your opponent lays down nothing—but reaches for the pot, grinning, 'Remember, my uncle is a Cardinal.'"

To Italians life is wonderful, living precious, tomorrow uncertain—and far, far off. Here, families are drenched with affection; they adore the children, love the parents, dote on siblings. Families eat together in the open—laughing and singing—at tables piled with bread, fruit, wine, cheeses, endless varieties of pasta. (Spaghetti, in case you have forgotten, came from China, via Marco Polo.)

"Italians are children," many an expatriate will tell you. Or: "Never believe a Roman: they are flatterers and wolves."

We know several American women, living in

Italy, who fell for some Latin who courted them, vowed undying love, smothered them with romance, bedded them, then wangled money on one or another pretext—and not once hinted he was married, or had three (or four or five) children.

One heiress told me: "Italian men are *incapable* of love. Oh, they fawn, they drool, they moan and moon. But they lie—how they lie! I have had three passionate swains tell me they would kill themselves if our great love was not to be. They took me to the cleaners. What a fool I've been!"

I asked her whether she had ever seen the movie *Summertime,* or read Tennessee Williams' *The Roman Spring of Mrs. Stone.*

She flushed. "Yes. Both. And yet—I love Rome. And I must try to live."

Until very recently, Italian law punished an adulteress severely, but not an adulterer. Aubrey Menen, who lives in Rome, says that Italians have always thought an immoral father better than no father at all. Besides, romantic love is just not taken seriously, except among the young. "In a country where there is no divorce, the condemned man eats a hearty meal. I have been the best man at many Italian weddings. The groom cries, not the bride."

The Italian language is so melodious that one walks down a Roman street as if through an opera. Besides, conversations in public are conducted

with theatrical exuberance, employing a vocabulary of gestures (hands, shoulders, head noddings
and shakings, eyes rolling in anguish or narrowing
in disgust) that make emotion visible. Sudden
sighs, cries, scornful shrugs and impulsive em-
braces make it possible for any viewer to enjoy
the drama of heart-to-heart talk.

A professor told Aubrey Menen that his Italian
was perfect—but wrong. "You speak Italian the
way you speak English: to convey ideas. *We* talk
to express the richness of our own creative gifts."

Italians garnish their utterances with oodles of
irony. Arguments start off with mock praises and
effusive compliments, then proceed to sharper ac-
rimony and naked insult. When cars scrape their
precious fenders, the drivers leap out and extol
each other's skill with *brìo*—before describing each
other's blindness, stupidity or ancestors. Such
eruptions attain added irony when conducted on
streets named The Sainted Fathers, The Sacred
Spirit, The Blessed Madonna.

You might ponder the fact that Rome's munici-
pal prison is called Regina Coeli: "Queen of
Heaven."

One night we clip-clopped through the moon-
washed streets in a horse-drawn carriage, born
through illuminations of the past: the Arch of
Titus, the Vestal Virgins' temple, the shards of the
Forum—that jumbled graveyard no one dares call
ugly (just as no one remembers that the Romans

hated to wear the toga). We drove around the fine statue of Marcus Aurelius, preserved because marauders thought it a statue of Constantine, the first Christian emperor, who doomed Rome's dominance when he moved the Holy See to the Bosphorus.

Another time, we drove down the Tiber, where the Castel Sant' Angelo (Hadrian's Tomb) looms. I wondered where Cleopatra had had her villa, and gave birth to Caesar's son. (She was far from being a beauty and was not Egyptian, but Macedonian.) The dome of St. Peter's soared into the sky, crowning a cathedral that overwhelms you by its scale and proportion.

I told my wife a story. Beyond the high altar in St. Peter's, four gigantic saints point to the golden throne. According to legend, Peter's Chair rests inside that throne. Years ago a most proper Englishwoman, Lady Morgan, asked the Vatican to open the throne, so that she might testify to the presence of St. Peter's Chair. The Church authorities—more astounded than offended—refused. So the lady wrote a book, in which she stated that on St. Peter's Chair is inscribed: "There is no God but God, and Mohammed is His Prophet."

Horrified, the Vatican reversed its decision and opened the golden throne. St. Peter's Chair was there, all right. And the inscription? Not a line is on the sacred seat. Lady Morgan had faked the Muslim litany to drive Catholic prelates up the wall.

H. V. Morton, who writes guide books one can read as if they are novels, said:

> The Rome that first prints itself upon the mind and eye is not classical Rome, buried beneath the streets . . . or medieval Rome . . . but this gay, declamatory Rome of the Popes, with its peachy, golden palaces, its once quiet piazzas, its glorious fountains, its look of just having happened on some fortunate day.

Rome is a city of statues and fountains. Water gushes even in tiny squares or alleys or shadowed courtyards: across dancing fauns, from spouting lions, down pagan gods, centaurs, satyrs, and all the bestiary of myth. Water splashes into bronze shells, down mossy grottoes, filling scalloped basins to cascade into larger urns and troughs.

The Trevi Fountain and its roaring falls are a magnet to tourists; but I never knew, until I read Morton, that the Trevi's triumphant Neptune faces a tiny church, across the small piazza, in which the hearts of twenty-two popes are preserved. Literally. In urns.

Statues stalk across Rome's skyline: apostles, saints, kings; martyrs and princes; a parade of figures appealing to heaven, kneeling, praying, turning, pointing, all the swirling robes and vestments caught in mid-motion.

Walk through Rome, and statues appear from nowhere—in a wall, a niche, on a pillar: Romulus and Remus suckling; a hundred Madonnas and a thousand Crucifixions; the busts of poets, popes, painters, composers; the heads of Gauls, Furies, boxers, discus throwers. . . . What city contains such lavish testaments to both its pagan and Christian past?

The afternoon light of Rome is unforgettable. If you sit in the Piazza Navona and gaze beyond the Fountain of the Rivers (its reclining figures represent the Nile, the Danube, the Ganges, the Rio de la Plata), you will see the fine stretch of buildings once occupied by Spanish ambassadors. At twilight, their plaster turns orange or rose.

The meadowed park on the Pincio Hill, with the palace of the Borghese at one end and the Villa Valadier at the other, is a fantasy at twilight. Here you may marvel over the panorama of Rome: palm trees and poplars and pines; below, the vast Piazza del Popolo, slashed by an obelisk from Egypt; the winding, tree-lined Tiber; the undulating Spanish Steps, brightened with umbrellas and flower carts; a cluster of church domes and bell towers. The other six hills of Rome are silhouetted against the horizon, and Michelangelo's dome makes St. Peter's a mirage.

Rome's sky is merry with swallows—swarms of them. They swoop in circles, cheeping shrilly. Some Romans tell you that if you listen closely you will hear that the "swifts" are not calling "Cheep-cheep" but "Gesù . . . Gesù . . . Gesù!" That, say the pious, is why the swallows always circle around church spires.

"All roads lead to Rome," the old saying went. The roads were thronged with pilgrims, sages, minstrels, priests. When they beheld the Eternal City, as Martin Luther once did, they burst into tribute:

> *O Roma nobilis, orbis et domina,*
> *Cunctarum urbium excellentissima.*

Cicero once wrote a friend: "Rome . . . the city, the city. Live in its full light! Residence elsewhere is eclipse and obscurity."

Imperial Rome ruled a dominion that stretched from Scotland and Spain to the Euphrates: 3,500,000 square miles. The Romans mastered mountains and marshes and African deserts. Their soldiers marched more than 100 miles a day. They built roads and temples, aqueducts, and amphitheaters that still astonish those who behold them.

The Caesars imposed the long peace of the *Pax Romana* upon a hodgepodge of states, tribes, religions, mystery cults. They were tolerant of any faith, so long as they stayed out of politics. Rome's genius for government civilized the West with a magisterial invention: Law.

The Roman mobs screamed homage to their legions, returning with priceless plunder from

Gaul, Egypt, Greece. Triumphant generals used to ride into the capital wearing laurel crowns, with their faces painted red, like Jupiter's. Haggard, vanquished people stumbled behind them: chieftains manacled, queens in fetters, and strange beasts in cages. The processional would mount the Capitoline Hill, where pagan sacrifices bloodied the altars to appease the gods. Once a year, a goose, clad in gold and purple, was carried around the Forum in a splendid litter. This commemorated the time the geese of Rome saved the capital by their honking, awakening the Romans to the fact that the besieging Gauls were trying to scale the hill. Thereafter, a dog was periodically crucified on a cross of elderwood and carried around in solemn parade—to remind the dogs, I suppose, that their ancestors failed to bark on the night the geese saved Rome from the barbarians.

Any schoolboy will tell you that the Caesars ruled by giving the populace "bread and circuses." But it was much more than that. Hear Polybius:

> What maintains the cohesion of the state is superstition. . . . Every multitude is fickle, full of lawless desires, unreasoned passion, and violent anger. [They] must be contained by invisible terrors and pageantry.

And what pageantry the Caesars (which meant kings, and gave us titles such as *kaiser* and *czar*)

put on to please the multitude! When Trajan de-
feated the Dacians, the celebration ran 123 days
and nights. When Titus dedicated the Coliseum,
in A.D. 80, a hundred festive days extolled the
event.

The Coliseum rose 150 feet above 80 huge
arches. It could hold 50,000 spectators. Vast colored awnings, rigged across the topmost tiers,
kept sun or rain from the howling crowd. Wild
beasts charged up ramps from cages beneath the
Coliseum's floors, which could be lowered or
raised for a spectacle—or even flooded for dra-
matized battles at sea. Corps of gladiators fought
on heaving decks, and "the water, lashed to
foam, turned red and fouled the flailing oars with
bobbing corpses."

Gladiators in the Coliseum fought to the death
with nailed knucklets, spears, spiked balls on
chains. They also battled bears, wolves, lions.
Blood-curdling ingenuity matched women against
dwarfs, wolves against zebras, lions against bears,
bulls against rhinoceroses.

Sometimes the arena was converted into a pas-
toral landscape, with trees, ravines and flowing
brooks; then naked captives were dragged in to
find shelter, if they could, from starved beasts of
prey.

The Romans gorged on food and wine as they
watched the gruesome spectacles; the Coliseum
rang with bet making on which human bait would

last longest. The horrible displays hardened the Roman heart, wrote Pliny the Younger, and taught them "to scorn death." They also scorned life. For Trajan's triumphant celebration over 11,000 beasts perished to please the Roman mobs.

So many hunters were employed throughout the empire, to capture exotic animals and ship them to the Eternal City, that in time no elephants were to be found in Libya, the Nile contained no more hippopotamuses, no lions survived in all of Greece.

The Roman theater could not compete with the public extravaganzas of torture and death. Horace complained that Roman audiences hooted the actors and demanded wrestling matches or battles between beasts instead. "Pleasure has moved to entertainment without meaning," he wrote. "Kings of fallen fortune are dragged onto the stage. War chariots hurry by. . . . All the spoils of Corinth are displayed. A giraffe catches the eyes of the crowd; or a white elephant. What actor's voice can carry above such a frightful din?"

The streets were filthy, the noise unbearable. Wagons crammed with timber and stone often tipped over, in roads meant for chariots, and crushed pedestrians by the score. The tumult of traffic was so fierce that Julius Caesar prohibited vehicles from using the streets from sunrise until five; this simply pushed the uproar into all the hours of the night. "Most of the sick perish for want of sleep," Juvenal reported; and Martial cried that he could not find a place to sleep or rest "for men as poor as I."

The proud city of marble mansions and golden temples was also a charnel house. Chamber pots emptied onto sidewalks; corpses were simply tossed into ditches, onto dumps, or into the Tiber—along with the bodies of executed criminals, assassinated rivals, and the carcasses of the beasts slain for public diversion. The Cloaca Maxima, a fourteen-foot-wide sewer carrying off the waste of the affluent, emptied into the Tiber, too. The putrefaction of corpses created such a stink that the authorities finally proscribed burials of any kind inside Rome's boundaries.

Our visions of the glory of Rome do not include such ghastly details. Nor do we remember that floods regularly turned the capital into a swamp, and the plagues took fearful tolls. Rome's physicians (usually Greek) did not know the cause of typhoid or malaria, raging fevers and endemic infections. The healers relied on magical potions, and counseled larger sacrifices to the gods. Whenever an epidemic struck, the rich fled the noxious city to villas in the hills, the mountains, beautiful Amalfi or Capri. But the people found no escape.

The wooden roofs of the city were coated with pitch, and fires broke out everywhere. Crassus made a fortune from his fire brigades; they would appear before a burning structure but made no move to use their hoses until Crassus bought the dwelling, at a bargain price, from the helpless owner.

Images of the past haunt my favorite museum in Rome: the Museo delle Terme, which inhabits the roofless shell of the immense Baths of Diocletian. On the denuded brick walls, once laden with porphyry and marble, six full storeys high, you can see (or imagine) where the lavish pools were set, where the fabled loggias and dining halls, the solariums and libraries.

I discovered the out-of-the-way entrance to the Museo years ago, and hurried to it on many a scorching day. The vast, deserted gardens, adorned with ancient sculpture, plaques, bas-relief, are a wonderful place to reconstruct the past. A building houses the Terme's treasures: mosaics removed from crumbling floors, exquisite frescoes, Greek statuary. To me, the most sensitive and appealing figure in the kingdom of art is the Venus of Cyrene. This headless, armless girl was discovered on an Aegean island but sixty years ago. She lacks only the decades of admiration showered on the Venuses of Milo or Medici.

Etruscan art glorifies the Villa Giulia, in an outlying part of Rome not familiar to tourists. The Etruscans and their culture remain a mystery to historians, for the most part, but this much I know: Etruscan art is one of the high-marks of civilization. Their attenuated statues (echoed today in Giacometti), their jewelry and artifacts, all agleam with the green-gold patina of centuries, are masterpieces of grace.

There is a terra-cotta sarcophagus in the Giulia on which recline a gilded, smiling couple, the man with a curly Etruscan beard, his wife in ringlets reminiscent of Egypt. The pair seem to signal that death need not end memories of love, and for a moment one thinks this marvelous couple not dead, but dreaming.

I write about the Terme and the Giulia because it seems pointless to sing yet another hosanna for the Sistine Chapel or the Palazzo Doria, the Raphael frescoes in the Vatican, Michelangelo's Moses, the stupendous colonnades of Bernini, the Pantheon's coffered dome. . . .

When I first came to Rome, it was a pleasant, quiet backwater of Europe, more museum than metropolis. Its tempo was lazy, its mood bemused. All was *dolce far nìente*. You could not find a clock, even in a bank or railway station, which considered time important enough to measure with exactness. The wide, leafy avenues contained but a few automobiles. The trolleys were quaint, rarely full, tinkling their bells to amuse the patrons at the sidewalk tables of lovely *trattorías*. Today . . .?

Today, Rome is monstrous. There is no other word. Those who wrote so lovingly of Rome (Byron, Goethe, Keats, the Brownings) would weep to see her now. The city verges on chaos, torn by endless strikes, paralyzed by an engorged bureaucracy.

It took my wife and me twenty minutes to get across one avenue, so thick and hostile was the torrent of autos, trucks, taxis, Vespas, buses. The stoplight was a joke. When we described the un-nerving episode to Jean Gavoni Salvadore, she laughed. "You must wait for a nun—or a pregnant woman—to cross. They are the only people our crazy drivers will slow down for."

Her husband, Lucca, grinned. "We are proud that you *never* hear of a nun or pregnant woman being run over."

Another night, we sat in an immobilized cab, trapped in a packed one-way alley with horns howling all around us—and fire engines scream-ing fruitlessly somewhere behind us, trying to get through to some fire ahead. I remembered the nightmare opening of Fellini's *8½*. In panic, it oc-curred to me that Rome is an asylum, the inmates locked inside throbbing vehicles, pounding on their horns, swearing at the world outside, raging to be set free. . . . We fled from the cab and hurried around the corner.

As for parking . . . ! Romans park wherever they want—double, triple, aslant, askew, on sidewalks, in courtyards. The widest thoroughfares become one-lane funnels. . . .

Our last night in Rome, we ate on the shrub-enclosed pavement before Passetto's. The pandemonium of horns and curses, the nauseating fumes, made us hasten back to our hotel.

I bolted the double windows. They diminished the city's roar—but we could still hear it. I turned on the television. I raised the volume. What did we hear? The pounding, yelling U.S. cavalry, chasing Indians who were uttering their war cries in (ye gods!) Italian.

I switched to another channel. "I Love Lucy." Once more I tried, and surrendered. "What's My Line?" (albeit with a cast of Italians) is not what I came to Rome for.

Early in this memoir I asked: "What can I say about Rome that has not been said a thousand times before?" I can say it now. The city has gone crazy. It scrapes your sensibilities raw.

I wonder if I shall ever come back.

☐　　　　　　　　　　　　　　　　　☐

ON AN
ALABASTER THRONE

Seventeen centuries before Christ, the civilization of Candia (Crete) was at the zenith of its brilliance. Three thousand six hundred and sixty-three years later, I sat on the alabaster throne in Knossos.

Sir Arthur Evans uncovered the palace in 1900. He called his archaeological treasure "Minoan," after mythical King Minos, son of Zeus (who was supposed to have been born on Crete).

The royal mansion was a wonder of huge stones and red, down-tapering columns topped by capitals of blue and gold. Deep within the palace was that maze of corridors known as the Labyrinth (the word is probably Egyptian) where the Minotaur, a ferocious bull, stayed imprisoned—and each year was fed Athenian youths from the best families. The only way to find the path out of the Labyrinth was by following a skein of thread, if you remember Vergil's *Aeneid*. It was great Theseus who finally slew the Minotaur.

All this is suggested in the exquisite frescoes of Knossos. They are marvels of grace: delicate flowers, flying dolphins, royal courtiers in diaphanous skirts. A bronze statue depicts a bullfighter grasping the Minotaur's horns and somersaulting above them in aerial bravado. I thought the most memorable piece of art a faience figurine of the Minoan cult goddess, the Earth Mother: tiny-waisted, bare-breasted, in a flounced-tier gown, a small leopard sitting on her head and a snake undulating in each hand.

Everything about Knossos is much smaller than I

had imagined. The Greeks were a short race. But heroic tales inflate the truth, and especially the pictures in our minds. Take the celebrated Throne Room. It is far below ground, and the "Alabaster Throne" stands against a fresco of lilies and two crouching griffins, who guard the royal seat. They are strange, playful griffins with peacock crests which remind you of Aubrey Beardsley or Art Nouveau.

The "Alabaster Throne . . ." How grand that sounds. But the alabaster is as mottled as old succotash, and the throne is a weatherbeaten slab with a high stone back and no arms. The hallowed seat did not flood me with awe.

Still, a throne is a throne; I plumped onto the adamant dais, bruising my coccyx but slightly.

My wife focused her camera. "You don't look Minoan," she complained.

"I won't put on a skirt!"

"How about a laurel wreath? Or a crown?"

"Do you have one handy?"

"Okay, put on your hat."

I donned my porkpie Panama.

"Look regal."

"A regal *shlemiel*, " I muttered, assuming as illustrious a posture as one can in a Marks and Spenser sport shirt dangling over Jamaican shorts.

"Don't sneer. Look majestic."

I felt dyspeptic.

"Click!" went the shutter.

"Oh, God!" moaned my bride.

Her irreverence was misplaced. The picture turned out dandy.

Whenever I feel lowly, not to say low, I fondly gaze upon that snapshot. How many boys from Chicago can say they sat on King Minos' alabaster throne? A less comfortable roost I have never known, but it is the only authentic throne which ever sanctified my bottom.

I left Crete grateful not to have been a Minoan, or even a king in Knossos: I live in a penthouse, not a basement, and my goose-down easy chair would have made Theseus drool.

Legends are the gussied-up gossip of the past.

☐   ☐

ESTORIL:
Glamour in Limbo

White mansions shine amidst the palms of Estoril, on the sea not far from Lisbon. Exotic flowers burst like rainbows over ornate urns, baroque gateways, sparkling stucco walls. Rolls-Royces drift along the fragrant avenues and occasionally a fringed surrey clop-clops down a dreamy lane. Old-fashioned straw hats adorn rich men in striped blazers and white flannels; pretty parasols shade the ladies who move—so elegant, so stately—across the marble terraces. Fountains splash soft melodies from a hundred hidden gardens.

I wanted to see Estoril (pronounce it "Esh-toréel") not only because it is lush and posh and beautiful. Portugal had long been a sanctuary for many an exiled king, dictator or royal pretender. They waited and waited and waited for fate to smile and recall them to one or another throne: King Carol of Romania and his mistress, Magda Lupescu; the dauphin claimant to the throne of France; that dissolute glutton, Farouk of Egypt; Don Juan de Borbón of Spain. . . . As the banished eminences gravitated to Estoril, they were joined by grand dukes and princes and hopeful junta generals. Royal blood attracts more than loyal seneschals: titled sycophants, wealthy leeches, ambitious dowagers, a gallery of paramours and consorts. As the sham courts dreamed of the glory they hoped one day to claim or reclaim, they whiled away the long, eventless nights with balls

and galas and—above all—gambling at the Grand
Casino.

An imperial assemblage, a heavenly climate,
plus a famous casino proved honey to the jaded
bees and drones of the world. So the creamy
hotels of Estoril played host to plutocrats and fortune hunters from all of Europe and Indonesia
and South America: tin-mine heirs, oil-rich sheiks,
movie moguls from Hollywood, London, Paris,
Rome. And the women . . . ! Princesses, courtesans, yearning widows from Palm Beach to Rio. It
was hardly surprising that so much lucre and li-
bido attracted gigolos from the Lido and the Côte
d'Azur and nearby Morocco.

Scores of splendid yachts dropped anchor off
Estoril, and ocean liners stopped over on luxury
tours. The Casino's launches sped to and from the
pleasure spot. And the local mansions bore the
flags of many nations, the standards of vanished
kingdoms and crumbled principalities.

✡✡✡

I had a special reason for wanting to see Estoril.
During World War II, Lisbon was the Mecca of
espionage, aswarm with agents of every conceivable power: German, British, Russian, French,
Italian, American. Agents and double-agents and
triple-crossers. Estoril was Lisbon's Casbah, so to
speak, rife with the razzle-dazzle of intrigue:
stolen weapon designs, clandestine meetings, dis-

creet garrotings. Estoril was a paradise for conspirators and con men.

At that time, I was a deputy director of the Office of War Information. At one point I sorely needed a certain Nazi movie, for a P.W. (psychological warfare) dingo in which I was involved. I asked the Army for help. G-2 asked O.S.S. The Nazi film happened to be playing in Lisbon—and that celluloid was duplicated, one night, the copy on my desk in Washington within fifty-four hours. (I never sneered at our cloak-and-dagger corps after that.)

After the war, I went to Hollywood to rewrite a melodramatic mish-mosh called *The Conspirators.* It starred Hedy Lamarr, Paul Henreid, Sydney Greenstreet, Peter Lorre—plus a fine cast of accented European players. The climax of the whodone-it erupted in the Casino in Estoril. . . . Can you blame me for wanting to see it?

I drove along the coast from Lisbon, lazed away some hours with the fishermen in Cascais ("Cashkai"), and went on to Estoril at twilight.

The Casino was virtually deserted: the well-heeled gamblers would not appear for several hours. So I had a drink and tried to strike up a conversation with one or another croupier. They were not blabbermouths—except for one, who seemed flattered to be interviewed. He said his

name was "Albuquerque." He was dark and sloe-
eyed, but otherwise bore not the slightest resemblance to George Raft. In fact, he looked more
like Merle Oberon.

"Gombling?" he leered. "Gombling is more better than love, *senhor.* This I can prove. To gomble
is—how you say?—to put spices in Life. . . . Also it
can make a miracle. You want I tell you one?"

I assured him I was a patsy for miracles.

"To this Casino came an English *homen,* a high-
born Lord, but sick, in a wheeling chair all the
time, pushed by servant. This Lord is with bad
pain all the times—from arathritis, a cripple, the
pains *patético* to see them. He does gomble.
Many times. . . . One night, this mon wins a
beeg, beeg sum in *roleta. Deus,* he is so excite he
jumps out from his wheeling chair! Without one
pain! Thot whole arathritis is disappear. He is a
cure! From gombling! How you like that?"

I demonstrated my astonishment so lavishly
that Albuquerque continued: "Also I tell you of a
fine professor of fame from Lisboa. A mon so full
with brain he does know *every*thing. There is no
more for this mon to know, is what all persons
say. One night he come here to Casino. To my
station. Ah, he is fascinate by *roleta.* I see this at
once. He cannot move the two eyes from my
wheel. He make no bet for much hours. He only
look, look, think, think, and is sweating soon like
a *porco.* Why, *senhor?!* Because he has find the
one thing *he cannot know:* 'What number will ar-

rive next?' . . . So he is coming back, all the time to my station, night follow night. Then he play. Very *audacioso,* much *bravata!"*

"Did he win?"

Albuquerque winced. "He lose. He lose all: money, auto, time-watch, everything what is in his bonk, his *casa,* even the jewels of his *mulher* which he has, how you say, not sell but—"

"Pawned?"

"Powned. And he lose. Everything!" Albuquerque grinned, exposing two front teeth of gold. "Still, you must know this: to gomble was for him the top of life! The climax, the *auge.* So in his *desperdício* it is worth all. For it excite his brain, his mind, his spice of Life—after he has so long think he did know all there is to know."

I asked Albuquerque whether different national-ities follow different patterns when gambling.

"Oh, *sim, sim!* To admire most, for me, are the English, mon or womons. So *correcto.* Much calm. *Coragem*—how you say, cowrage. Such *re-visão* of the face." He made a bleak poker face. "Not the once he did show feeling: good, bad, of despair, of the victory. . . . Ah, the English. Is to odmire."

"What about the French?"

He wigwagged a scornful hand. "Some this, some thos. Baddy loser. *Not* like English."

"The Italians?"

He sneered. *"Italianos?* They made much Sign of Cross, they pray God; and when lose, they cry like the baby. But when win—*Deus,* they make as men crazy! *Louco!"*

"The Germans?"

He spat on the floor. "Who does feel *simpático* for them? The eyes go *rã-rã"* (*rã* is Portuguese for "frog") "the mon go anger, those *gordura,* fat womons"—he pantomimed a pair of mammoth breasts—"are as to die from a lose!"

"What about Americans?"

He hesitated. "You *Americano,* nao?"

"Don't let that bother you."

He wrinkled his nose. *"Desculpa, senhor,* excuse. American is not good gombler. Oh, they play for small *dinheiro,* few dollar, and smoke the many cigarette and make bod joke, all the time talk-talk-talk. They *show* the every mood. I regret to admit you all this."

"I appreciate your honesty."

"Graças."

"How do you feel about your work? All you see and hear?"

"La vida," he shrugged. "Life is not to understood, *senhor.* Full tricks. How explain *destino?* One day is anchor here thot famouse ship S.S. *Caronia,* eh? This ship which makes the trip around world, with only *milionários.* It cost, I am hear, twenty t'ousand dollar—American!—for one accommodation! So our boats go from Estoril to this big ship, and bring the everyone here from *Caronia.* They come in the Casino, beautiful in the clothes, the jewels, the fine furs. And they

play." He slapped his cheek. "It is not to believe it! *Every single one does win!* Such a night hos never be see here before! The lucks have conspire, I tell you. Two hondred t'ousands *'scudos* the Casino hos lost thot night! All to *milionários, senhor!* . . . Before they come, we think so much *milionários* will be the chonce of the life for the Casino, no? But—Pfft! They pick the tables clean—blackjacks, *roleta, Le Craps*—clean, like feathers from *frango*—how you say, 'chicken.' Who can explain such a thing? The poor, the little mon, with few money, he only hope to win a little—and *perda!* He lose. But those *milionários*—! They can *burn* moneys—and *ai, ai, ai! They* win! Almost the whole Casino they did win in thot once!"

A party of six came in, three couples, causing a flurry among the attendants. I recognized one of the men, Federico de M., a Spaniard with whom I had lunched several times at the Jockey Club in Madrid. He waved to me and bent over to whisper to the woman who appeared to be hostess. She was in her forties, striking, elegantly dressed and coiffed, puffing a thin cigar through a long ivory holder. Whenever she flicked the ash off the cigar, light sparkled from the gems on her wrist.

Federico came over to me. *"Amigo!"* We shook hands. He said, "The Contessa asks will you join us for an *aperitif?"*

That I did, bowing to each member of the group during Federico's introduction, and kissing the

Contessa's hand. (The way she extended it made a buss obligatory.)

The talk was cocktail trivia. "I saw her with that hideous Brazilian. . . ." "How was your tennis?" . . . "They're off for the Algarve tomorrow. . . ." "Oh, *do* tell the story of the cat to Francesca. . . ."

My perfumed hostess turned to me, away from the others. "So. You like Portugal?"

"Very much."

"Why?"

I uttered a few banalities.

The Contessa waved them aside. "Politeness, politeness. I will inform you, my friend. You cannot deny this. We, in Portugal—we are not a beautiful people. No, no, do not stop me. We are small, and swarth, and given to hair. Our women are thick. Our men smell of pomades. Such men?! Oh, they are so conceited! Name of a name, it is not to believe! When a Portuguese man looks on a woman, do you know what he says to himself? *I* know, for often I have heard the men making little jokes among themself. The Portuguese man thinks: 'That lady is glancing my way. Ah, she cannot keep her eyes away from my charm. She is pining for my attention. She needs I should deliver her from such desolation. Perhaps I should be generous—thrill her, why not? So. I will look into her eyes. I will regard her with amour. . . . Ah, she is flushing now, radiating joy, so grateful. . . . Ah, I am inflaming her sense! She is wild for my possession!' " The Contessa clucked. "That is how they think! Is that not disgust-making?! *Senhor,* do gentlemen in America act so? Think so? Like foolish *chouriço?"*

I gave her my solemn assurance that gentlemen in America never think or act like *chouriço.* I did not know what *chouriço* meant, but I knew American males do not behave that way.

To Federico, I later whispered, "What does *chouriço* mean?"

He canopied his lips with his hand. "Sausage."

Have I let you down? I went to Estoril as to a fable. What I found was what I found in Las Vegas or Monte Carlo: the rich and the spoiled, fending off the most debilitating of human ailments—boredom.

HYDE PARK HASSLE

When I learned that three English friends had been trying to reach us at our fancy hotel overlooking the leafy green of Hyde Park, leaving their numbers (we had received not a single message, much less an actual phone call), I stalked into the office of the manager. He looked like a bloated David Niven.

"Astonishing," he sighed. "Of course, we *do* have a bit of difficulty with new telephone personnel"—he lowered his voice—"some are Maltese. But I shall issue strict orders at once! I assure you, sir, this absurd situation will be remedied."

I don't know what he meant by "remedied," but we received nary a phone call or message that day. We fumed in what is aptly called frustration.

My wife said, "Go down to the lobby. Pick up a house phone. Ask for Leo Rosten. I'll bet they don't know we're registered."

I hastened down to the cathedral lobby and did as instructed. "Leo Rosten, please."

"*Would* you mind repeating the name, sir?" a charming Duchess asked.

I repeated my name.

Pause. "How is that spelled?"

Slowly I spelled out: "*R* for 'robber,' *o* for 'oboe,' *s* for 'spy,' *t* for 'tomato,' *e* for 'Elizabeth,' *n* for—'Napoleon.' "

"Thank you, sir. One moment please."

Fifty-three moments later, I heard: "I'm frightfully sorry, sir, but *no* one of that name is registered."

"I *know* he's registered!"

"Really?" A sniff skewered my self-esteem. "Are you certain?"

"I am *quite* certain. I happen to be Mr. Rosten!"

The phone went dead. It stayed dead. . . .

I stepped to the next house phone, into which I bleated: "Mr. Rosten, please, Leo Rosten."

A Caribbean refugee replied, "Could you please spell thot?"

"Gladly. *R* for 'Roman,' *o* for—'osteopath,' *s* for 'sex,' *t* for 'tattoo,' *e* for 'Easter,' *n* for 'Newton Abbey.' "

"One mo*ment*, please. . . . Oh, sir, thot name does not oppear in our—"

I accosted an assistant manager. "Can you help me? I'm afraid your telephone operators just don't understand my American accent. Would you mind phoning the room of Mr. Leo Rosten: *R* for 'Roosevelt,' *o* for 'Oglethorpe,' *s* for 'stupid,' *t* for 'thermometer' . . ."

He lifted both a disapproving eyebrow and an incriminating phone. He asked for my room. . . .

"What? . . . Oh." He frowned, covering the phone with his palm. "Are you *shaw* your party is in the hotel?"

"Absolutely shaw. In fact, you are looking at him."

He flinched. "Do you mean you are trying to ring *yourself*, sir?"

"I am trying to get my wife, who is waiting at the phone right now."

The man's face burst into ecstasy: "Ah, then you know your room number."

Steelily, I showed him my key.

He lifted the phone with confidence. "Room faw-one-six, please." He handed me the receiver.

"*Hullo-o-o,*" came a hoarse Nigerian bass.

"Is this room four-sixteen?" I asked.

"No! Thees room is foh-foh-seven."

I replaced the phone on the cradle. The assistant manager had evaporated. I tried to think peaceful thoughts. Instead I churned up homicidal impulses. . . . Then sweet inspiration struck me.

I lifted the phone yet once more. "I want to leave a message, please. . . . Thank you. . . Would you take a message for Room four-one-six? For Mr. Leo Rosten. . . . Just tell him that Prince Rupert of Albania telephoned."

And that night, for the first time, a chit from the Telephone Message Center was slipped under our door. It read:

"Mr. Leo from Boston called. He is on his way to Rumania."

THE VALLEY OF THE BUTTERFLIES

We drove to the Valley of the Butterflies, on the island of Rhodes, and walked up a narrow trail shaded by tall trees. Soon we entered the special stillness found only in woods. At a hut in a clearing, the Greek guardian of this glen greeted us, led us further into a sylvan declivity, where the filtered light made mosaics, and stopped. The grove lay heavy with silence.

"Observe trees—not leafs—*trees*," he said.

The barks of the trees were lavishly mottled, like some Aegean variety of eucalyptus, all dun brown, flecked with pale, pale green.

The guide put two fingers into his mouth and blew a shrill, piercing whistle. Before our eyes a fury of whirring wings materialized: every tree was stripped clean of its mottled "bark" and the air flickered dark with butterflies—ten thousand, twenty, thirty? Every trunk's outer layer had peeled off and rushed upwards, a vast armada of winged things whirling in frantic circlings.

The great swarm clouded out the sun for a moment, and we stood in thrall to the hum of thousands of beating wings. In less than a minute, the insect cloud dropped down and away, as swiftly as it had soared, and the ghostly butterflies returned in separate multitudes to the tree trunks, where they settled, absolutely inert, mottling the trunks brown-green once more with their folded wings.

The guide smiled, "Is beautiful?"

We were speechless.

The guide put his finger to his lips, signaling us

to remain silent. After a while he clapped his hands sharply, twice, and again conjured up the astonishing spectacle. Every tree's dappled bark peeled off, skybound, to form a massive, mothy, whirling canopy; and the immensity of wings beat out an angry, bee-like buzzing. The butterflies wheeled above us in that huge, dense congregation, making the light flicker and dance across our upturned faces.

When the throng dropped down and divided in battalions to perch upon the trees, the woods fell absolutely silent once more, and the shafts of sunlight were not streaked with winged shadows. . . .

We waited, expecting the guide to produce the miracle again, but he shook his head. "No soon. Let rest. Let rest."

In this haven, not visible from any hill or road, on this Aegean island near Anatolia, this fortress-isle so rich in tales of Saracens and the Crusader Knights Hospitaliers of St. John, the dun butterflies slept in their hidden valley.

□   □

UNION SQUARE

Union Square used to be the Hyde Park Speakers'
Corner of New York, jammed with soap-boxers,
hecklers, evangelists and caterwaulers, political
demonstrations and passionate debates. I once
heard two morose Italians, dressed in their Sunday "best" (dark suits, white washable ties, velour
hats), talking quietly on the fringes of a crowd that
was listening to an atheist's harangue. I have
never forgotten their colloquy:

FIRST MAN
How you wana die? Lak a *man,* no?

SECOND MAN
I no care how die.

FIRST MAN
You *musta* care! Isa two kine die: Gooda die anda
bada die.

SECOND MAN
Is no gooda die.

FIRST MAN
Isa gooda die! Man laya downa bed—closa da
eye, nice, calma. Laka he sleep. He no breathe.
He joosta—die. . . . Datsa gooda die.

SECOND MAN
(staring at pavement)
Die is alla same.

FIRST MAN
Is *no* alla same! Whassa matter you? Ina war—

thatsa bada die. . . . How you like I com, pusha you lake thees—(imitating a bayonet thrust) *oomph!* Ina belly. Maka you blod jump out—like squeeze tomato. You choka. You drowna. In own blod. . . . *Datsa* kine die you lak?

SECOND MAN
(dully)

Die is die.

□   □

HOW I DID NOT PHOTOGRAPH LENIN'S TOMB

I doubt whether it would happen today. But it did, years ago. In Stalin's Moscow.

I wanted to take a picture of Lenin's Tomb. You would think that about as eventful as taking a shot of Grant's Tomb. You would be wrong. For at the time I visited the Soviet Union every foreigner received an official pamphlet of ominous Do's and Don'ts; and among the sites sternly forbidden to cameras were bridges (however small), marching soldiers (however few), "military forts, installations, *or any parts or portions thereof.*" The Russians had such a mania about espionage that even the outside of the Kremlin was off limits to photographers.

Now, Lenin's Tomb is in Red Square directly in front of one flank of the wall which surrounds the Kremlin. To photograph the sacred mausoleum without including a piece of that wall is not easy. You can aim your camera very close to the Tomb, of course. But I had a movie camera and wanted a moving shot, advancing from a panoramic view of Red Square to a close shot of the shrine where Vladimir Ilyich lies miraculously embalmed.

I decided to run no risks. I wrote a formal application, through Intourist, to the Minister of Information, asking permission for a long-to-close-up shot of Lenin's maroon marbled sepulcher.

Days passed without a word of response. Each morning I asked the man from Intourist about my application. Each day he beamed, "Soony, soony."

After five days it occurred to me that "Soony, soony" might easily mean "Don't be silly." I thereupon informed Intourist's agent that I had not until now wanted to use political pressure, but I thought that his superiors ought to be told that I was the President of the United States' favorite nephew, a godson of the Chairman of the Senate Committee on Military Appropriations, and was at this very moment writing a book entitled *Who Are America's Real Friends?* and subtitled *My personal experiences in the U.S.S.R.*

That did it. As in any dictatorship, threats plus insolence strike terror into the heart of any bureaucrat.

The next morning, exuding good tidings and sour perspiration, the Intourist agent rushed into my hotel with an embossed envelope. Within it I found—well, not exactly Official Permission, but an encouraging and potent *aide-mémoire:* If esteemed Professor Leo Rosten of the U.S. of A. would appear "at guard station in Kremlin Tower" at exactly 16:00 hour, "an Official Permit to allow photograph Lenin's Tomb, observing proper respect for laws and regulations by military authority of Kremlin Guard," would there be forthcoming.

At 15:00 I set off. By 15:30 I was in Red Square. According to my guidebook, there are no less than seventeen Towers rising from the Kremlin Wall. To which Kremlin Guard station should I present my friendly features? Feverishly, I reread the communiqué from Intourist. It helped me not.

I hurried to one Tower, where an extremely humorless soldier barred my entrance. A Captain bolted out of the guardhouse. I smiled appeasingly. I presented my letter. The officer emitted a torrent of emphatic *"Kak dnyevesti pozhalypta!"*'s (I render my phonetic impressions, making no claim whatsoever as to meaning). The officer sneered and signaled me to go leftward, which is not my political inclination.

The Tower to the left proved to be the one where potential saboteurs such as I had to report. A soldier under a sign, *Vkhod* ("Entrance"), slanted his rifle at a 45 degree angle, thus directing me to a door, which I entered.

I found myself inside the guards' dressing and sulking quarters. The room contained a stove (center), a desk (right), a bench (left), three pictures on the wall (Marx, Lenin, Stalin), and a pendulum clock above a shabby door which led to a room (or cell) beyond.

At the desk, a Lieutenant rose, lowering a cigarette with one hand as he placed the other in the pocket of his jodhpurs. His jacket was casually unbuttoned at the throat. He was so debonair that he made me think of Fredric March's Count Vronsky, in *Anna Karenina*. Unfortunately, he smiled, exposing a picket fence of lead-and-steel teeth. *"Tovarishch?"* He inclined his crew cut courteously.

"I was told to come here," I said, slowly and distinctly, "for a pass—to take pictures of Lenin's Tomb."

The Lieutenant looked puzzled. *"Tovarishch, ponimaete po-russkoj?"*

"N-no; but this letter from Intourist. . . ."

The Lieutenant's perusal of my paper was accompanied by pitying snorts which suggested that it was not a paper whose contents he held in high regard. He frowned. *"Tovarishch, pon-i-maete po-russkoj?"*

"No. . . . *Parlez-vous français?"*

He looked buffaloed.

"Sprechen sie Deutsch?" I ventured.

Vronsky did not deign to deny comprehension of the Huns' detestable tongue. He stared at me. I tried to look as sympathetic to the glorious Soviet Union as possible. I grinned. I chuckled. I—

Lieutenant Vronsky pressed a button. The door behind him promptly opened and two soldiers, pistols in their ugly holsters, lunged in. They snapped to attention. Vronsky spoke to the underlings. One of them nodded crisply. *"Tovarishch,"* he asked me, *"pon-i-maete po-russk-oj?"* I suppose his dialect was so different from his Lieutenant's that the latter hoped I would understand the patois of the former.

I shook my head in shame.

The trio frowned: first at each other, then at me.

I thrashed about for a solution. "Intourist!" I cried. "Call *Intourist—telephono—Intourist!"*

The Lieutenant went "Ah!" and lifted the phone. *"Intouristi!"* roared my reborn Vronsky. *"Kak metdshn pzartma koi?"* (I flinched.)

In twenty minutes, almighty Intourist appeared—in the form of a short, pretty girl wearing
the inevitable emblem on the inevitable beret.
She also had the inevitable hairy legs. It took her
but a moment to scan my *pis'mo* ("letter") and
comprehend my *vopros* ("question"). Followed a
rapid exchange between the indignant Intouristi
and the bristling Lieutenant, garnished with con-
trapuntal explanations, defensive maneuvers, and
defiant quotations from the Party Literature. At
last Vronsky initialed a white card which contained three facsimile signatures and a Hammer
and Sickle. The hammer looked stronger than the
sickle.

"Everything is arrange," Miss Intourist told me.
"Now, please to listen. Remember, comrade, take
picture only of Lenin Tomb. *Not* Kremlin Wall,
not even small *piece* yet of Kremlin Wall!"

I will not pretend that my response was diplomatic. "The whole damn *point* in my applying," I
seethed, "was to get permission to start with a
long shot which *does* include a piece of the holy
Kremlin Tower, the sacred Kremlin Wall, the
sainted Kremlin niches. When I report this idiotic
ruling to Washington. . . ."

And because it was not diplomatic but bullying,
my tirade frightened the quartet.

The Lieutenant appealed to the Girl Scout to
protect him from my wrath or, at least, to remember that he was neutral. He did not like Siberia.

She soothed me with sweet tidings. *"Da, da,*
professor. I will take you by myself! I accompany

to make possible to you this permission!" She turned to the Lieutenant and in a spate of Slavic communicated my special need, shaking the *pis'mo* ("letter") before his perfectly normal *glasa* ("eye").

He flung his hands up.

She put her foot down.

He gave her a vulpine leer.

She lowered a coy eyelash.

He smirked.

She smiled.

He scribbled something on the white card under the Hammer and Sickle. *"Khorosho,"* he crooned.

"Spasibo," she murmured.

I was so elated that I offered to sight each of them through my finder. They could scarcely believe their good fortune. I raised my camera and peered through the viewfinder. Mind you, I did not start the motor; I just peeked through the viewfinder. Vronsky promptly drew erect, posing like a Grand Duke. I "panned" to the guards, who stood as frozen as if they were, and to blushing Miss Intourist. *"Khorosho!"* I exclaimed.

Now joy reigned so unconfined that I handed the camera to Vronsky (covering the motor button with its safety tab). He blinked at the instrument with dignity, then focused on me. *"Zhrob kno bubyanitze!"*

"What?"

"He say to—to make a formal pose."

I am ashamed to tell you that before I knew what I was doing, I had turned my hat sidewards and thrust my hand between the buttons of my shirt. "Napoleon . . ."

The soldiers burst into applause. The Lieutenant flung a hearty arm around my shoulders. Miss Intourist demanded to know whether in capitalist countries such fun was possible for the downtrodden proletariat.

Lieutenant Vronsky thrust out his hand. *"Do svidaniya, Tovarishch!"*

"Do svidaniya." I clasped his hand.

"Do svidaniya, tovarishch!" The soldiers saluted.

"Do svidaniya, tovarishchi!" I three-fingered back.

"Some day *every* worker will have camera!" cried Miss Intourist.

I opened the door, in love with the world, the Kremlin, the guards, a Higher Cultural Level for the Proletariat. I halted.

It was pouring.

THE GIRL IN RHODES

She sold sandals in a small shop in Rhodes. She was not much older than eleven. Her blouse was faded, her skirt skimpy. Her skin was sallow, her hair unbrushed. But she was as bright, as cheerful and infectious, as any child I ever knew. Her smile lighted up the shop. Her laugh, as she showed us slippers and sandals, was irresistible. And we, in our innocence, caused her great grief. . . .

Rhodes is the emerald in that necklace of twelve isles known as the Dodecanese. Asia Minor is but a dozen miles away. The ancient Greeks named the island Rhodos: "Bride of the Sun"; the Italians dubbed it "The Island of Roses." This fertile haven in the Aegean, aburst with flowers and fruit and sweet scents, is blessed by breezes that temper the sun.

You sail into the harbor straight toward the high medieval wall which once surrounded the city. The huge stone blocks are crowned by slits and serrations from which the archers sent down their arrows. Beyond, you catch tantalizing glimpses of a Muslim minaret, a Byzantine dome, a flurry of spires and steeples that testify to Christendom.

Around your ship flirt coveys of fishing craft, an occasional felucca or dhow, pretty caïques flashing their rainbowed sails. Sunburnt boys and sunparched men fish off the long quay to the north. They often pound octopuses to death on the rocks (at least forty times, lore demands, to be sure the creatures are dead). On the waterfront, you see garments which remind you of this island's jumbled history: Greek shirts, Arab headgear, beaded blouses, a Turkish fez, curve-tipped sandals, turbans, dresses with a kind of embroidery once found only on Rhodes. The mélange of garb is nowhere as ornate as it sounds, for the people who live on Rhodes are far from rich.

The *Delos* dropped anchor south of the two long parallel quays, where, straddling the old entrance to the harbor, one foot on each of the quays, stood the Colossus, that stupendous bronze statue of Helios, the Sun God, over 100 feet tall, one of the Seven Wonders of the World.

In Greek mythology, Rhodos was the daughter of Helios and Venus, the bride given to the Sun by Zeus himself. Ancient documents tell us that a mirror on the breast of Colossus was so immense that it dazzled seamen off Egypt, 200 miles away. But nothing remains of the famous behemoth— not a foot, a toe, a knuckle.

The recorded history of Rhodes begins a thousand years before Christ. This stronghold between Anatolia and Alexandria, facing Asia Minor on one side and Africa on the other, once a great sea power, was invaded and conquered by the Persians, Greeks, Romans (Rhodes unfortunately sided with Pompey, so after Caesar was assassinated, the "lean and hungry" Cassius arrived to plunder the errant islanders), the Saracens, the Crusader Knights Hospitaliers of St. John (who made it their bastion), the Turks, the Italians, the Germans in World War II. . . . Each sovereignty left some mark on "The Sun's Bride."

We spent ten cloudless summer days on Rhodes, in a white villa on the beach fifteen miles beyond the city of Rhodes, into which we wandered every afternoon. In the "Old City" the names of the shops are inscribed in Greek or Turkish. Here old men wear towels around their heads and smoke hookahs, and old women's skins are very dark and dry, as creased as parchment. The half-Gothic arcades are cool; and down the cobblestone streets stride priests of the Eastern Orthodox Rite, or the Coptic (Christian-Egyptian) Church, in thick, black beards, high cylindrical hats, long black cassocks.

The dwellings are jumbled together here, their colors faded into pastels: pinks and peach and lemon; a hyacinth doorway, a garden wall splotched cinnamon; pale violet gates, casements of bleached purple. You glimpse tiles from Istanbul or Iran, Moorish ornaments, canvas surely dyed in Marrakesh. The scene sings in stippled light, light that filters through overhead trellises of rush or vine, through slanting colored glass or arbors of bougainvillaea. . . .

Whenever we rambled through the Old Quarter, I thought of the haunting dream cities Klee painted, scenes he named Vol or Prhun or Air-

Tsu-Dni. The names are meaningless, the pictures unforgettable.

The heart of the Old City is the famous Street of the Templars (more properly, the Knights Hospitaliers of St. John of Jerusalem), where the buildings are fortresses with nail-studded doors, windows crisscrossed by iron, great gonfalons and curving sconces. Nearby is the Mosque of Sultan Mustafa, and the Byzantine church of Saint Phanouries. In the Museum courtyard, stone cannonballs, four inches thick, are piled in neat pyramids. Occasionally, we heard the thin, distant wail of a muezzin, summoning Islam's faithful to prayer.

⁜⁜⁜

One day we drove out to the Bay of Lindos, and I swam in the most beautiful blue lagoon—a half-moon pool of sea, half a mile wide—imaginable. It is no small thing to float on your back and behold a magnificent Acropolis, crowning the high headland, its creamy pillars and broken pediment a stage-set against the Aegean sky.

We rode home across the spine of interior hills, across very dry, hot country, down dusty roads to villages where life is lived out of doors, where the men sip ouzo and skinny dogs trot after half-naked children at play. The grizzled, fierce-mustached elders play cards all day long under rickety lattices; the women all wear black dresses and swathe their hair in peasant kerchiefs. Goats and donkeys roam about freely, and shepherds cross the barren, unpaved squares with live lambs slung around their shoulders.

In a street in modern Rhodes we finally found a shoe store. Native sandals and beach shoes filled the window. We went in.

The proprietor was plumped on a battered kitchen chair. He was swarthy, potbellied, and as heavy-lidded as a frog. The stub of a brown cigarette hung from his lower lip. He did not rise. He grunted something in Greek. At once, a girl appeared through a beaded curtain. She greeted us with a most radiant smile and liquid Greek phrases. She was small, slender, wearing a frayed blouse and an ill-fitting cotton dress. Her skin was pallid, her hair hung plain, but her eyes were as bright as a robin's. She laughed as she signaled us toward chairs, kneeled, removed my wife's shoes, and swiftly brought her beach sandals and canvas loafers. The smile never left the girl's lips as she trilled phrases of praise about the footgear—even after it was clear that we did not understand a word.

She hung on the English we exchanged as if by sheer effort she could decipher the meaning. Her eyes kept darting to my wife's necklace and earrings.

My wife said, "They're not jewels. . . . Not *real*, you understand? We call them—'junk' jewelry."

The girl glanced at the proprietor.

"She not undrestond," he grunted. "No school."

"Is she your daughter?" I asked.

"Óchi," he snorted. "No. Is only work me." He translated my wife's words about "junk jewelry" to the girl. Her hand flew to her mouth; she burst into laughter and bubbled her unbelief that such beautiful adornments could be cheap.

When my wife indicated that she wanted to buy one pair of beach slippers, the girl clapped her hands like a child, sped behind a counter and wrapped the shoes. After she gave the package to me, she stood quite erect, her hands behind her back.

I paid the proprietor.

The girl darted toward the door, bowing and laughing, *"Efcharistó . . . efcharistó."*

The next night, after dinner, we found ourselves passing the shoe store again. There was a new display in the window. Some espadrilles caught my fancy.

The moment we entered the shop, the girl broke into that childish laugh of delight.

I said to the proprietor, "In your window. . . ."

He grunted to the girl, who darted out to the sidewalk and beckoned me to show her which style I wanted to see. I wigwagged through the window.

The girl hurried back, searched the shelves,

pulled out a box. She bubbled cheerful phrases in Greek all the while, as if she were acting out a song.

Suddenly, my wife blurted: "Let's buy her a decent dress!"

I thought of our own daughter in her graduation gown. "Sure." I asked the proprietor if he would let the girl come with us for half an hour or so. "We'd like to buy her a present."

He shrugged.

"What's her name?" asked my wife.

"Marina."

"Tell her we want to give her a dress."

The proprietor fingered his cigarette stub and told the girl. Her mouth dropped. She reddened in total astonishment. She put her hands to her cheeks, as if to arrest her blushes. Then she curtseyed.

When we left the shop, the girl hurried us around the corner, chattering like a peewit. She stopped before a window filled with fabrics: bolts of cotton, linen, silk in a profusion of colors and prints.

"Don't you want a *dress?*" my wife asked in surprise, pointing to her own.

A flood of merry syllables accompanied Marina's head shaking; she pantomimed the act of guiding fabric under the needle of a sewing machine, pumping her foot and intoning, *"Singer . . . machina . . . machina! . . . Singer . . ."*

They went into the store. I watched them

through the windows. The girl went from one counter to another, her eyes devouring that feast of colors and designs. She would point to a bolt, and my wife or a clerk would hold a portion of the fabric against the girl's body or up to her cheek.

At last they came to the doorway carrying two bolts of silk; Marina held one swath, then the other, close against her body.

"They're both pretty," I said.

My wife and the girl went through a comedy of communication, my wife saying, "Nice? . . . Lovely? Which one you like?" and Marina draping first one then the other print across her breastless figure.

"Which do you like best?" my wife asked me.

"Hell," I said, "buy her both."

My wife said, "Marina . . . " and held both bolts together. "Both." She held up two fingers. "Two . . . *due* . . ." Marina's hand flew to her mouth. She flung her arms around my wife and kissed her, hugged her, then turned to me, blushing, uncertain whether to hug me, too.

I bent down. She pecked my cheek. *"Efcharistó! Oh, efcharistó!"*

The day came for us to leave the beach and Rhodes. A taxi drove us into town. The *Delos* had arrived again that morning. We were to board her at seven and complete the circuit tour—to Santorini, Crete, back to her home port, Piraeus.

My wife said, "Let's stop, just a moment—to say good-bye to the girl."

We found the street easily. The proprietor was standing in the doorway. The brown, dead cigarette butt was pasted on his lower lip. He nodded.

"We thought we'd say good-bye to Marina," I said.

The frog shrugged. "No here."

"Oh. Is she coming back soon?"

"No. She home. No work here more."

My wife frowned. "Why? What happened?"

The fat shoulders hunched up. "You buy her silk—for dress, *né*? . . . So next morning, girl's *mitréra*—mother—comes, pulling her like animal through street. Girl is crying. Mother much angry. Demands me to talk. She do no believe girl, who tells how two Americans did buy this fine silk for dress. *'Why?'* asks Mother. I say to her is just *dóron*, how you say—present. Mother spit. 'One was *man?! What my girl gave?! What she promise? Why a man gives girl such *dóron?!'* Marina talks and cry—but is no good. Mother slap-slap face. Girl cry, 'I good girl! No do bad!' " The proprietor picked the dead stub off his lip and studied it in disgust. "That is how it is with poor."

"But didn't you explain?" asked my wife.

He shrugged. "I explain, *né*, but this Mother spit, 'You lie also?! You play with my girl's'—how you say . . ." he fumbled for the word.

"Virtue," I said miserably.

"*Né*. Virtue."

"Where do they live?" asked my wife.

The *Delos* hooted from the harbor.

"Perhaps *we* can explain—"

Again that exasperating shrug. "What explain? The woman ask, 'They did *touch* my girl?' I say, 'But in nice way. Like mother, like father.' But she scream and pulls girl out, like goat, slap her, pull her through street, shout bad names on her. . . . This is the way with poor."

The *Delos* hoarsely growled.

We stood at the rail as the ship slipped away in the fading light, the pitted medieval walls receding slowly, the citadel of Romans and Saracens and Crusader Knights drifting back into the distance as if into the dead past itself. We stood at the rail a long while.

"They say the Colossus stood right there . . ." I began. It was pointless.

We could not bring ourselves to talk about the girl in the shop.

□   □

THE SAD, SAD FADOS

Machado's is a cabaret, famed among Lisbonese (more accurately: Lisboans) who love the *fados*.

Fado means fate; but *fados* are the special, schmaltzy, gloomy songs the Portuguese adore. They listen to elaborations of misery hour after hour, wallowing in wine and *Weltschmerz* and exercising the lumps in their throats.

The *fados* are unlike any popular ditties you ever heard. Sometimes stylized, sometimes spontaneous, they always recount doleful troubles and doomed amours, maudlin crises and galloping despair.

This night, in the smoke haze of Machado's, a plump, pneumatic contralto moaned her tales of agony to the accompaniment of a guitarist whose skill with the strings was overshadowed by an expression worthy of Buster Keaton with a bellyache.

Our host, an enthusiastic masochist, translated the unforgettable (I wish they weren't) words of one *fado*. I do not claim that what follows is an exact rendition, but it's close enough to give you the mood of the Portuguese blues.

THE ACCURSED LOVER

Overture

Woe is me
Oh me, oh my,
Let this tale
Dim ear and eye.

Canto

I once was lovely, sweet and innocent,
Bright of smile and even thinnocent,
Until the day—oh, God, to think—
He paused beside our kitchen sink,
And gravely glanced into my eyes,
Ignoring mama's soup and pies,
To whisper, "I love you, dear . . ."

Reprise

Woe is me,
You know by now,
I fell from grace
And—well, and how!

Elegy

How we loved and how we laughed,
In the moonlight on a raft,
Drifting nowhere in our passions
Kissing, loving, nothing rationed.

Recitative

Can you guess it, or believe—
How that man did me deceive
To my bed he never tarried
Nor did tell that he was married!

Coda

O, woe is me
Farewell, my virtue.
Dear God: I didn't want
To sin or hurt you!

□   □

THE PRIDE OF PALERMO

How long had I yearned to see Sicily, that gleaming island tipping the Strait of Messina, so rich in legend, so ravaged by history, crowned by snow-sloped Mount Etna and Taormina, a jewel of resorts.

The capital, Palermo, was one of the great cities of the world in the twelfth century, an Arabic emirate renowned for her Byzantine churches, her luxurious palaces and Moorish gardens. Agrigento, in the hilly south shore, still boasts the finest (surely the best-preserved) Greek temples in the world.

Sicily: the ancients called it Trinacria, because of its triangular shape. The Phoenicians settled the coast eight hundred years before Christ. For centuries thereafter, this lush isle between the Ionian and Tyrrhenian seas was a prize—besieged, invaded, conquered by the fleets of Greece, Carthage, Rome.

When the dominion of each expired, a host of new dynasts invaded Sicily: Goths, Papists, Normans. Scarcely a pirate or madman in the Mediterranean spared the island's tempting riches. The Spaniards, the French, the Hapsburgs—in turn, each coveted and conquered the strategically placed appendage to Italy. Sicily bears the mark of each and all of them. And of the Mafia. No one in Sicily forgets the Mafia. It is the infragovernment of the countryside.

Such jumbled oddments tossed in my mind as we drove from the airport to Palermo late one summer night. I had insisted on a large room with a balcony that faced directly on the sea.

The sleek Swiss chieftain of the Hotel Jolly (you read it right) ushered us into our quarters. He drew the draperies apart proudly. "Most beautiful view in Palermo!"

A fragrant breeze wafted around us, but since the night was moonless all we could see was a sea of darkness.

"In the morning, *signor e signorina,* you will find the beach almost at your feet! This sight, I assure you, is one not soon to forget."

We dined in our room. A buxom chambermaid with the face of a benevolent Borgia turned down our beds and closed the draperies. They drifted in that sinuous breeze, and throughout our impatient dreams.

Came the morn. Before I even rang for our breakfast, I swept aside the draperies and stepped out to the balcony. The Swiss major-domo was right. It was a sight no one would soon forget.

"Come see our superlative view," I called.

My wife hastened to my side. And gasped.

We broke into laughter—outraged, but still laughter—for we beheld: beach chairs. Empty beach chairs. Five rows deep. Crowded together. Canvas beach chairs. Plastic beach chairs. Nylon beach chairs. Beach chairs of every conceivable shape and form. Beach chairs with arms, beach chairs without arms. High-backed beach chairs, low-backed beach chairs. Beach chairs with wooden frames, beach chairs with aluminum muscles. Beach chairs bottomed near the sand, beach chairs bottomed high above it. Beach chairs with canopies, beach chairs with curtains.

The conglomeration of shapes and sizes was matched by the array of weaves. Some beach chairs were solid, some were webbed. Some were slatted, some were checkered. And the variety of weavings had reason to blush beside the rioting of colors. Red beach chairs, blue beach chairs, red-and-blue-and-green beach chairs. Colors solid, colors striped, colors splotched, colors cross-hatched. Colors—well, it was a Sicilian carnival arranged by a drunken upholsterer.

Those damn beach chairs blotted out every inch of the deserted golden (I assume) sands of the "most beautiful" (I imagine) beach. It was only beyond the bizarre bazaar that the Tyrrhenian Sea, mocking us, glittered its liquid diamonds.

The beach chairs were not meant for occupancy, mind you. They were the proud *pièce de résistance* of the International Beach Chair Exposition, which was honoring historic Palermo with its annual display that lucky year. I'll bet you didn't even know there is an International Beach Chair Association. *Mihi crede.*

We left for Taormina the next day.

□   □

THE DOUKHOBORS
OF MEXICO

I had this very rich friend Percy (he hated the name) who lived on the crest of the Hollywood hills in a scrumptious home with a panoramic view of the San Fernando Valley. Sometimes I stayed with him. He was a marvelous host.

Percy had inherited a discombobulating amount of money. His grandfather had built a string of movie theaters from Santa Barbara up through Morro Bay and Fresno into San Francisco; his grandmother had inherited half a mile of dirt land that became the Sunset Strip. Percy had had a kid sister, Dawn, who crashed her private plane into a row of bungalows in Culver City. That left Percy the sole heir to the family fortune.

He was quite handsome—tall, lean, always tan, a Barrymore profile. He was also very strong. Barbells and pulleys filled a spare bedroom he called "The Gym." He exercised even when relaxing, flexing a rubber bone in one hand, then the other. He liked to put two walnuts in his hand and crack them by squeezing. I once saw him tear a telephone book in half. The population of Oxnard was nowhere as large as it is today, so the directory was nowhere as thick. (I say Oxnard because that is where he tore the phone book in half.)

Percy had married the daughter of a famous wildcatter, but the union did not last. She ran away with his best friend. Percy rarely talked about her, but when he did he called her "The Snake."

Many of my friends in L.A. wondered how I

could spend time with Percy. They thought him a bit of a bore. I didn't. I found him a delightful companion. He had an altogether unique, offbeat sense of humor. He was funny in a way I have not encountered in anyone else. He would start telling you something, throw off a provocative line— and stop. The stop forced you to ask a question, which was exactly what he wanted so that he could floor you with an answer out of left field. He was very clever about conning you into a question. And soon I found myself using the same style whenever we were together. Our conversation resembled verbal Ping-Pong.

I don't suppose I would ever have seen a Doukhobor if not for Percy.

One day we were at his pool watching a Technicolor sunset, over our drinks, just the two of us, and he sang out, "How would you like to visit some Doukhobors?"

"Doukhobors are among my favorite birds."

"Doukhobors are not a bird, buster. They are a human—very quiet and gentle. They are a religious sect. They began in Russia but live mostly in Canada. The men wear beards. They all go around naked a lot."

"Canada is a long way to go to see men in beards and naked Russians," I said.

"I did not say we have to go to Canada to see these Doukhobors. There is a colony of them tucked away in a certain mountain near Enseñada. A four–five hour drive from here."

"What on earth are they doing in Mexico?"

"I don't know. Their parents fled there, I guess. The Doukhobors were persecuted wherever they roamed. They are sweet, peaceful people. They began like Quakers, except for going around naked. The ones in Enseñada belong to a group that split away from the group in Canada." He ate a pretzel. Percy was always munching on something or other, but mostly on pretzels. He had them stacked in apothecary jars all around his house. "What are you doing tomorrow?"

"I'm going to the studio."

"Which studio?"

"Warner Brothers. Right down where you're looking."

"What are you going to do there?"

"I am going to write a scene or two for a screenplay."

"I didn't know you had written a screenplay."

"I haven't. I'm working on one."

"I hope you sell it," said Percy.

"I don't have to sell it. In fact, I couldn't sell it if I wanted to."

"Why not?"

"Because Warner Brothers is paying me to write it. Every page I scribble is their property. When the script is finished, it will belong to them and they'll start to make a movie and I'll leave you and go back home."

"Yeah."

"I told you all this when I moved in," I said.

"That's true."

"So why do you act surprised every time I tell it to you?"

"I forget," said Percy.

"What do you forget?"

"I forgot what I forget." He grinned. He had been putting me on. "Still, I'd like you to see those Doukhobors."

"Why?"

"I don't know. They're nice people. It's a nice ride."

"Have you been there before?"

"Sure. Lots of times. They like me."

"Do you speak Russian, Percy?"

"No, I don't speak Russian."

"I assume the Doukhobors speak English."

"Nope."

"Then how do you communicate?"

He shrugged. "We say hello and smile and they make signs for do I want a drink (only water or tea, you know; they *never* touch booze), some bread and sour cream, vegetable chow. . . . Then I look around with Moses—he's their leader—to see what's happened since I was there last, and maybe play with a kid or two, although that gets nowhere because they're so shy with an outsider; and then I drive back. . . . You really ought to see some Doukhobors before you die."

"I'm not planning to die for a while."

"Well, before I die," said Percy. "If I kick the

bucket, you'll probably never get to see a Doukhobor."

"Oh, I don't know. You've whet my appetite. I might drive down there one day on my own."

He grinned, "Oh, no. That's where I've got you by the short hairs. You don't know where they are."

"In Enseñada."

"They're *not* in Enseñada."

"You said—"

"I said they were in a certain mountain hideout in the mountains *near* Enseñada. Hell, Mac, you could go to Enseñada and ask the ten leading *caballeros* in town to tell you where you can find the Doukhobors. They'd think you were loco. I'm the only one you'll ever know who can lead you to them."

"How did you find them in the first place?"

"Some day I'll tell you. . . . What about it? I'll do the driving. You can enjoy the scenery."

"How do you get there?"

"The coast road, straight down the coast, through San D. and across the border to Tijuana. Have you ever seen Tijuana?"

"No."

He looked disgusted. "I'll be damned. I thought you liked to travel."

"I do."

"Then how can you turn down a chance to see picturesque Tijuana?"

"Is it that beautiful?"

"Hell, it's not beautiful at all. It's picturesque. A bordertown, honky-tonk, full of Mexican whores and sharpies, tourist creeps from the States. Lots of saloons and shops. You can buy anything from fake pre-Columbian jewelry to authentic stolen jockstraps."

"You make it sound fascinating."

"We won't stop there long. We go through it into *Baja*."

"Another architectural gem?"

"Naw. *Baja* means 'lower'—Lower California, the Mexican peninsula that hangs down below San Diego like a long appendix. All we do in Tijuana is soak up a little foreign atmosphere. Then we head for Enseñada. . . . Only, I'll give you one hint," he winked. "We don't go *into* Enseñada. We turn off, into the mountains, at a certain place before. . . . What do you say? Tomorrow morning. . . . You know I hate to go anywhere alone."

After dinner, Percy practiced fancy shots on the billiard table in his game room. I went into his library and looked up the Doukhobors in an encyclopedia.

The word in Russian means "spirit wrestlers." They are Eastern Orthodox Churchers, but reject the idea of any priesthood. They also oppose state authority. They believe in absolute equality and frugality. They think armies are sinful, so they refuse to be conscripted. The Czars persecuted them. In 1899, Tolstoy helped them get out of

Russia—to Saskatchewan. Around seven thousand men, women and children made the journey. It's amazing how little I know about things like that.

The Doukhobors were fine farmers in Canada. They built their own roads and dug their own irrigation systems. Their farms flourished, their orchards bloomed, and they lived in a total commune, sharing everything. And, of course, they schismed. One group split away, calling themselves "Sons of Freedom." Their most startling credal novelty was nudism, which also was their most effective political weapon. They used to take off all their clothes and march in front of Saskatchewan's government buildings whenever they wanted action or to protest against some impending legislation.

I wondered what branch of the Doukhobors Percy's belonged to.

We drove down the coast road in Percy's blue Cadillac and it was very sunny and lovely. In Laguna we lunched at a restaurant, right on the Pacific, with a beautiful big terrace on top of a riot of geraniums, red and white, thicker than I had ever seen.

Percy took off his blazer. He was wearing a short-sleeve shirt and his muscles glowed in the sunlight. He saw a luscious blonde at a table near us, with an older woman, and he waved to them and grinned and said "Excuse me" and went over to talk to them. Soon they were all laughing. He came back in a few minutes and scribbled something in the gold-edged memo book from Dunhill's he always carried.

"Friends?" I asked.

"Mother and daughter."

"But you know them?"

"Sure." He grinned.

"I mean did you know them before?"

"Naw. But I told them it certainly was a surprise to see them again. If you say 'again' it puts them on the spot. They don't want to come right out and ask exactly where you met them."

"What did you say?"

"What I always say. 'At Sally's.' Or 'At Mike's.' Soon we're making small talk, and I say 'I'll call you when I give my next big Hollywood party. Sally and Mike will be there.' So they give you their phone number. . . . Actually, the mother is sexier than the daughter, in my opinion. What do you think?"

"I think you're crazy."

"Stick to the point, chum. Do you prefer the blonde to her mother?"

"Yes."

"Gentlemen prefer blondes," he said, and slapped the table.

He was a clown, all right, but his heart was as big as all outdoors, which is where we were eating at the time.

As soon as we crossed the border at Tijuana, Percy began to sing "South of the Border." After that, he choked up on "In Old Monterey."

Tijuana certainly lived up to Percy's description. It was a border town: bawdy, rather decrepit, crowded and noisy. The streets were lined with saloons and lawyers' offices. From what I gathered, the lawyers offered Americans quick divorces and non-Americans visas or help with U.S. Immigration. I saw a bullfight poster and a few drunks sleeping on the sidewalk.

"Imagine a town full of sombreros and peasant peekaboo blouses this close to home." Percy pulled up and parked before a saloon with swinging doors. "Let's have some beer. Ever drink *cerveza?*"

"In Spain."

"Mexican beer is better. It ranks with the best beer in Germany."

The name of the saloon, I regret to tell you, was Las Cucarachas. *Cucarachas* sounds very romantic, but it means "cockroaches," which are not.

The dive was not too crowded, but sounded slaphappy. It had a certain ratty charm, I suppose. The floor was covered with sawdust, all right, and brass spittoons reminded you that in this very den of iniquity real he-men once spit into urns. There was a huge glass behind the bar, on which flamenco dancers were painted in pretty ghastly colors by some epileptic hophead.

The walls pleased me because they were covered with old movie posters bearing Spanish titles: Dolores del Rio, Leo Carrillo, Rod la Rocque (would you believe it?)—and a real beaut of Paul Muni, I think, in *Juarez*. I say "I think" because the artwork on the poster was so lousy it was hard to tell. From one angle Juarez looked like Paul Muni; from another he looked like Dorothy Lamour.

The bar had an ornate rail and a mahogany top with the antique effect bestowed by old alcohol stains and burned cigarette marks like worms. The bartender wore garters on his striped sleeves, his shirt had no collar, and the rag he used to dry the counter resembled a Jackson Pollock. *"Buenos días, señores."*

"Buenos días," said Percy gravely. "Where's the boss?"

"You want I call thee boss?" asked Garters.

"Sí. Thee boss."

"You know heem?"

Percy raised his closed fore- and middle-finger. "Like that. We went to Yale together."

The barman turned and called toward a curtain of leather strippings. I expected Peter Lorre to come through. Instead, I got Roy Rogers. A Latin, moon-faced Roy Rogers, about fifty years old. He had a pair of handlebar moustaches, and his hair was parted exactly in the middle and slicked down with Vaseline or something in a way Roy Rogers would never have approved of. It was hard to believe such a hairdo in a place this close to home.

"Pancho!" said Percy.

"Pearcy!" said Pancho, grinning like a split sausage. "You old some of a gun, *mucho tiempo* no see."

I saw what kind of a treat I was in for. Pancho was as much of a comic as Percy.

"Hey, dope," Pancho scowled at Garters. "What you waiting for? Two beeg mugs for my two best friends. . . . Pearcy, *amigo*, how you bean?"

"Jumping."

They both burst into laughter. I couldn't figure out why, until Percy chuckled, *sotto voce*. "He always says *'bean.'* Get it?"

"Jumping—beans," I said.

"Now you're cooking."

"I suppose that's one of the things you learned at Yale."

"Who said I went to Yale?"

"You did."

"Not to you! To the dummy. . . . Pancho, meet this gringo. His name is León."

"*Ponce* de León?" Pancho cackled.

We shook hands.

Garters slid two large, cold beaded mugs toward us, and a third to our host, who raised his mug and said, "*Salud!*"

"*Salud,*" said I.

"Do not drink yet! *Salud, pesetas y amor, y tiempo para disfrutarlas!*"

"That's real nice," said Percy.

We drank. The beer was very cold and malty. In fact, it was perfect.

"*Salud, pesetas y amor, y tiempo—*" Percy repeated dreamily. "Man. That's the best toast in the world: 'Here's to love and money and plenty of time to enjoy them.'"

"Pearcy, it is true good to see you *otra vez* sober. How long you were here before? *Long* time."

"I never count my blessings," said Percy. "How's your gorgeous wife?"

"Like a *mujer.*" Pancho stuck out a hand and tilted it back and forth. "One day happy, one day dumps. What you can do? . . . Hey, how's about this beautiful one you bring here last time? That was some piece *ai-ai-ai.*" Pancho's hands carved Raquel Welch out of the air. "This one was the most sweet-patooty *muchacha* I ever see you with."

"She's around."

"She is *mucho* round!" cried Pancho. "That one has not one flat place on her *cuerpo*, Pearcy. . . . Two more *cerveza*, dope! Wake up, wake up. Here are two *amigos* I go to hell for. Hey, León, now *we* talk. What you do?"

"He sells midgets," Percy cut in.

"What is midgets? For machines?"

"Midgets are very, very small people. So high."

Percy bent low to show Pancho how high. "León finds them and sells them to circuses."

"To *circus?!*" Pancho whistled. "Some of a beetch!" He winked at me. "This Pearcy. Always the jokes. Crazy *chistes*. Never he can be serious man for serious talk."

The brilliance of the repartee was giving me a headache. "I thought we had a date with some Doukhobors," I said.

"Right."

Percy paid Pancho for the beer the two *amigos* he would go to hell for had consumed.

"*Adiós*, Pearcy. *Adiós*, León." Pancho followed us out through the swinging doors, massaging his handlebars as he uttered effusions: "Go in healthiness! Drive with thee saints! I pray the Madonna to bless thees blue car! Comm back soon! Comm back. *Hasta luego! Hasta luego!*"

The last thing he yelled, waving farewell as we drove away, was, "May God give you plenty chickens!"

Those were the last beautiful words I heard in picturesque Tijuana.

"Boy, that Pancho," Percy chortled. "Isn't he something?"

"He sure is something," I yawned. The beer was making me sleepy. So was Percy.

"I've brought a stack of chicks into his joint, including the Snake, who *hated* him, and I'll bet you he can describe each one of them to a 'T.' "

I groaned. "Do you mind if I nap?"

"Shoot."

"Shoot" isn't exactly the best word to use in agreement to someone's taking a nap, but I had become accustomed to Percy's lingo and dozed off without correcting his diction.

I slept blissfully.

Several hours later the car exploded. A bomb went off. Right under my seat. I bolted out of my slumbers.

Percy winced. "Boulder. Sorry. This is a real rough road, *amigo.*"

I looked at the road. It wasn't a road. It was a double rut, lined with big stones and pitted with deep holes.

The next hour was like being in a washing machine that had burned out its bearings. We bumped and bounced and rattled something terrible. My stomach kept hitting my Adam's apple. I felt as if I was being massaged from the inside.

"I assume this is the best road to Doukhobor Haven," I gasped.

"*Si.* It is also the only one."

A cannon tore holes in the underside of the Cadillac.

"I think you should stop before there isn't one bolt left in this beautiful car."

"The idea is good," said Percy. "I usually stop about here—and walk the rest of the way."

"I'd rather walk than be torn to pieces."

"You are a good companion and a tough *hombre.*" He killed the motor and we walked.

It wasn't easy. That path was meant for the

wagons and carts of the Doukhobors. Between the boulders, the stones, the holes and the manure, I could hardly wait to lie down.

We must have been up fifteen hundred feet when we heard someone calling to us. Percy cupped his mouth and yelled "He-lo-o-o!"

We trudged on, breathing heavily. Two children ran down a path toward us, their eyes as big as oranges, and stopped on an outcropping of rock to stare at us. They were very serious.

"Hello, Ivan!" called Percy. "Hello, Sonya."

"You know their names?" I asked.

"Naw. I call all the boys Ivan and all the girls Sonya. Hey, there's Moses!"

I beheld a tall, bearded man. He was wearing a Russian peasant blouse and his trousers were tucked into his boots. Percy hurried up and pumped the old man's hand. *"Tovarishch! Great to see you again!"*

The old man smiled and spoke a few soft Russian words.

"Absolutely!" said Percy. "This is my friend—*mi amigo.* Shake his hand."

I shook hands with Moses.

"How is everything?" asked Percy. "Hey there, Alexi!" He began to pump the hand of another bearded man who had come out of a log cabin. "Where's your old lady? Babushka!"

A woman stepped shyly out of the cabin, several naked children clinging to her long skirt. She was wearing a babushka, all right.

Soon we were surrounded by Doukhobors.

They nodded gravely and studied us—our clothes, our faces, our shoes—as if we had dropped down from Mars. The children scurried in and out to take a swift glance at the strange visitors. They did not come close to us. They did not chatter or giggle, as children do. They were clean and solemn.

Moses said something to one of the women, who turned and disappeared into a hut. When she came out she was carrying a pitcher of water, and another woman was carrying a tureen of soup. They set the pitcher and the tureen on a crude wooden table on the porch of a cabin.

"Wait'll you taste their food!" Percy grinned.

Moses beckoned us to the plank benches at the table. Another woman brought a large loaf of black bread and a big knife. Then a fourth woman put tin spoons and forks before us.

The soup was not *haute cuisine*. But the bread smelled like honey.

"How *about* this grub?" asked Percy.

"Excellent."

"Every damn thing is home made! The food. The huts. The table. The benches. . . . They have a little church, over there."

The Doukhobors stood in a row before the balustrade of the porch and watched us eat. They said nothing. When I caught the eye of a man, he would nod. When I caught the eye of a woman, she would lower her head.

"Takes you out of our tawdry, materialistic

world, doesn't it?" Percy narrowed his eyes to show he was being philosophical.

"It certainly does," I said.

They brought us a copper samovar and we had steaming glasses of tea. Percy took a cube of sugar and dipped it into the tea and sucked on it. "This is the way Russians who are *really* Russians sweeten their tea."

"You certainly are a Slavophile," I said.

"The hell I am. I just like these people. They're for real. Honest. Kind. The world would be a better place if there were more like them."

"That's for sure."

"If I had any guts," said Percy, "if I really had the courage of my convictions, I'd get converted. Yep. I'd grow a beard and bring a good woman up here and raise a family and spend my life far, far from all that phony tinsel in Hollywood!"

"You would?" I asked.

"Naw. . . . Did you really think the blonde in Laguna was sexier than her mother?"

"No."

He wiped his mouth with his handkerchief. "Okay, let's put it to a test. When we get back, I'll phone those two snakes and I'll bang them and I'll let you know which one is really better between the sheets."

"You certainly would make a prize convert to the Doukhobors."

"They don't understand a word we're saying. Let's go."

We stood up and Percy said to Moses, "Anything new around here? Any new building or anything?" His hand made a generous arc.

The old man bowed slightly and led us around the village. There were not more than two dozen cabins, so far as I could see, but several were large dormitories, with bunks in them. Everything was very simple, very clean, very sparse.

Percy looked at his watch. "We'd better shove off. . . . Well, so long, Moses. It's been *wonderful* seeing you again. Thanks a million! The food was delicious."

We shook hands with Moses and with several men. The women stayed in the background.

As we left, Percy went over to the table where we had eaten and slipped some money under one of the glasses. Moses protested (I gathered) but Percy put his arm around the old man's shoulder and squeezed him. "You keep it. Buy something for the kids. See you soon. *Do svidaniya!*"

"*Adiós,*" said Moses gravely.

We stumbled down the rutted path. Cloudlets of dust trailed behind us.

It took us half an hour to drive back to some sort of paved road, and in ten or fifteen minutes we reached a highway, and Percy, looking as fresh as a daisy, stepped on the accelerator.

He sighed with enormous contentment. "What did you think of my Doukhobors?"

"Very moving."

"I shouldn't stay away so long. I love them."

"Why don't you join them?"

"Don't be silly. They're nice, but I think they'd bore me after a while. Don't you?"

"Yup," I said. "They certainly would. May I be perfectly frank with you?"

"Sure. Shoot."

"You ought to leave your brain to science."

"Oh, I don't know. I'm not especially smart."

"That's why you ought to leave your brain to science. They have lots of brains of geniuses, memory freaks, lightning adders-and-multipliers; but I'll bet they don't have one brain even remotely like yours."

"I'll think it over. . . . You know, chum, you are a true friend. True blue. No one in my life ever thought I ought to leave my head to science. If I decide to do it, what medical school should I put in my will?"

I couldn't think of the institution right away that deserved Percy's brain. "Any booby hatch will do."

Percy sank back in the seat and began to sing "La Paloma." He stopped after the first line. "Listen, pal. Tell me the truth. That cheesecake in Laguna. Did you *really* think the mother was sexier than the daughter?"

□   □

TERROR
AT UBEHEBE

Our genes make us mountain people or meadow folk, children of the desert or communicants of the sea. I spend much of my life on the beach; but I have never lost my astonishment on first beholding a desert.

I had read Doughty's *Arabia Deserta* and Lawrence's *Seven Pillars of Wisdom*. I was prepared for the special magic of desert air and light. But when I first beheld Arizona, I knew that nothing in words could convey the altogether strange beauty of sand and sky, the blazing sun and mirific moon, the wildflowers which colored that barrenness stretched "yonder all before me . . . in vast eternity."

I went each year for a decade to the Mojave, or the deserts of Nevada, or to what was then unchic, uncelebrated Palm Springs. I used to drive to Cathedral City (an absurd name for a gas station and a few adobe shacks) and would take one of the dirt roads under the canopies of palm trees, driving to the very end, where the road met a deep, wide arroyo.

I would leave the car and cross the arroyo (always dry when I was there; torrential "flash floods" sometimes drown unwary desert voyagers) and climb up the farther bank. The snow peaks of San Jacinto crowned mile upon mile of undulating sand, a great dry ocean of ripples and waves. Then I wandered in that bewitching isolation.

A desert glitters with tiny diamond granules and

"fool's gold" and fragments of varicolored stone that should be as precious as they look. In Arizona and New Mexico, the horizon is spiked by saguaros, which stand like figures incinerated in moments of agony. In the California deserts, tumbleweeds roll with the wind, hollow barbed balls with smoky strands; and barrel cacti, mesquite, wiry-fingered *ocotillo* dot the land.

The desert sky is a blank shield, but at twilight the sun splashes exotic hues across the heavens—pink, lilac, orange and, at last, purple, when darkness abruptly falls. In moonlight, a pale enchantment deifies the theater of this world.

There are no sounds on the desert, most of the time, no sounds at all. But a howling wind sometimes swirls the sand into a storm—and you had better flee it, for it blinds you, burns your lips, stuffs your ears and nostrils with grit, claws into every crease or juncture of your body.

I said no sounds ordinarily disturb the desert's silence; but that is not entirely true. If you listen you may just hear—then see—the scuttling of some tiny creature into a hole that closes behind it in a swift funneling of sand. Bizarre creatures live in the infecund grit: beaded lizards, snakes, chameleons, and Gila ("Heela") monsters. These dragons of the desert are enough to freeze your blood when you first come upon one. The head is flat as a crocodile's, the jaws long, the eyes ghastly, the scaly body splotched with tubercles, the toes clawed, the tail prehensile. This lizard family (Heloderms) is poisonous, but their bite is not fatal to man. They are creatures of nightmare, meant for old wives' myths.

The most fearful place I can remember is north of the Mojave: Death Valley. That destitute land is the lowest spot in the Western Hemisphere (280 feet below sea level). Mount Whitney towers 15,000 feet not a hundred miles away. The Forty-Niners named this moraine Death Valley because so many seekers of gold died there, of thirst and exposure, shriveled by the fire of the sun.

The declivity between the Panamint and Amargosa ranges is an inferno in summer, when the temperature reaches 125 (it has soared to 134), but in winter, a sort of summer reigns in Death Valley, and it was then I ventured into the canyon. I had charted my course beforehand, delighted by names like Skidoo, Hell's Gate, Stovepipe Wells.

The landscape was unlike any I had ever seen: pale promontories, all their colors bleached out save for borax streaks and ashy dirt, the sand baked to hard clay, sudden abutments striated by burned-out yellow and umber. The bald slopes of Funeral Mountain accented the eerie desolation.

We do not think of time as visible, yet here the signature of time stabs your eyes: harsh scratchings in walls cut by the claws of the winds, pockmarks on surfaces shrunk and cracked by the ferocious heat.

Ubehebe Crater was where I was heading. No one knows what "Ubehebe" means; all that is clear is that it is a Shoshoni Indian word. I always feel frustrated when I cannot find the origin of a word, annoyed by the failure of our ancestors to note a meaning or derivation. Words are such wonderful things.

"Ubehebe . . . Ubehebe . . ." Hypothetical images, pure onomatopoeia, teased my mind: an Aztec god, whose worshippers had been driven north by Cortez, and performed their hideous sacrifices in this canyon; the Navajo word for throwing a poisoned spear; Congolese for lips flattened into plates. . . . The game is amusing—if you have someone to play it with. "Ubehebe. . . . Ubehebe. . . . Ubehebe!" Hell, it sounded like a Cheyenne describing a chugging locomotive.

As I drove across the desiccated moonscape, I began to feel uneasy. I had not seen a rabbit, a bird, a lizard on a rock along the roadbed. Ahead loomed—a curve of clay-walled dead end.

Suddenly a shadow fell, quite early in the afternoon, and it was cooler—cooler and more ominous, for a wind began to moan. I was tempted to turn back. "Damn Ubehebe. This is far enough. . . . Don't be a fool. . . . " I drove on.

The road ended. No sign, no trestle. The grading of the rolled road just stopped.

I got out of the car. To the left was a mounting slope of slag: charred, cindered coke. I clambered up the clinkers, tripping, sliding back; the crackling of scoria under my boots sounded like protests, as if I were smashing bones from some incremated monster whose ghost held vigil and cursed my desecration. ("Don't be silly!")

I was breathing hard when I reached the top of

the charcoal slope. I was at the crater's rim. I gazed down, down—into an immense, charred bowl, some eight hundred feet deep, the guide-books had said. Here a volcano had burned itself out.

I had been to the top of Vesuvius, when I was in my twenties, seen the steamy spume pouring from the inner cone. The air was acrid. Under my shoes, through cracks in the cinders, I had seen red-hot lava, an underground stream moving very slowly, like thick red oil. I had taken a stick and poked into the coke and pulled up a blob of lava, which I put on a rock. I had dropped an Italian coin into the lava, which curled around it, bend-ing it, then, cooling, turned brownish-black. . . . I had used the coin in the dead lava for years as a paperweight, until a maid threw it into a pailful of fireplace ashes, and dumped it all into an ashcan in the alley.

But here. . . . No smoke, no steam, no lava, no acrid air. Nothing but the horrid stillness of that deep, black bowl. I stared into the dead abyss. An extraordinary passage from Nietzsche surged out of memory:

> Whoever fights monsters should be careful not to turn into a monster himself. When you look into an abyss, the abyss also looks into you.

The sun's shadow was a shroud. The wind began to blow, moaning a dirge, stinging my cheeks with sharp grains of grit.

"The abyss looks into you. . . ." I tore my eyes from that damned black hollow, that cemetery in a bowl. Suddenly, I felt as if I was the only remaining man in the world—as if the entire world beyond the mountains which surrounded me had been obliterated, obliterated while I was driving through Death Valley.

I drove back at insane speed, hating and fearing that accursed wasteland, praying for the sight of something living—a rattlesnake, for all I cared—or the miracle of a human presence: a hitchhiker, a camper, the crummiest prospector. But there was nothing. No one. Nothing. Not even a skull had survived the carnage of the sun. No raven screeched. Only those satanic shapes of clay bounced back the screech of my tires, like ghouls keening.

A sliver of moon punctured the sky. From every escarpment, shadows clutched toward me. Finally I saw the magic of light bulbs, distant signs of the living: Furnace Creek Inn.

I slammed down on the accelerator, skidded, churned up a cloud of ashy powder. The car tipped like a buckboard wagon, two wheels in the air, two scouring out a ditch beside the road before all four bounced back, shuddering. . . .

There was no one at the bar of the Inn, so I rattled a swizzlestick against a glass until Borax Bill, the cornball master of libations, appeared. He was wearing an old ten-gallon hat and a fancy cowboy shirt. "Howdy, pardner, and what'll it be?"

"Martini."

"*One* gut-burner comin' up! . . . Hey, what's the matter? You look like you seen a ghost."

He poured the drink, chuckling. He poured it deftly, to the very brim of the glass, and when I picked it up my hand was trembling. The glass was shaped like the crater.

□　　　　　　　　　　　　　　　　□

TIPSY-TOES IN TOKYO

We flew home from Kyoto, having arranged to spend the three-hour layover in Tokyo's neat little airport hotel. There we bathed and rested and talked of the marvels we had beheld in this enchanting land.

My wife sighed, "I'd give anything for a massage. Before we get on that long, long flight—just think of it. A massage."

I picked up the phone with a flourish.

Within five minutes, a dapper, smiling hotel official guided the masseur into our room. The former led the latter to my loved one's bed. Both of them were beaming and bowing. The masseur was blind. That did not surprise us. In Japan, the massaging profession is, most astutely, reserved for the sightless. What did surprise us was that the massage-giver was male. Every previous practitioner of the art before whom we had lain—in Kyoto, Nara, Kurashiki—had been a woman. Usually fat, always grinny, unfailingly excellent.

The hotel man suggested to my wife, "Prease to upset honorable self. Prace face in pirrow."

My wife turned over, "upsetting" herself, placing face in pillow, purring in anticipation.

The hotel man made his sayonara, bowing and hissing and backing out as if I were the King of Siam.

Grinning, and grunting Nippon's gutturals of esteem, the masseur promptly shed his slippers, jumped on the bed, and proceeded to walk up and down my wife's spine. That was the way he was massaging her. His delicate feet and twinkly little toes minuetted up and down her spine.

"*Omigod!*" gasped my bride.

I said nothing. How could I? I was choking.

"Stop!" my wife begged. "Tell him" (gasp) "to *stop!*"

"No speak Yopenese," I gurgled.

"He's *killing* me!" croaked Mrs. Rosten-san.

"A walking massage is the best kind Japan offers," I observed.

"*Hai! Hai!*" barked the masseur, who thought we were extolling his talents.

"Oof! . . . *Oomp!*" my loved one responded to the pedestrian ministrations.

"I wish I had a camera handy," I said. "I wish I could capture this moment and preserve it for our grandchildren—"

I stopped, puzzled. My wife's squeaks and squawks had subsided; indeed, they had turned into cooings of unalloyed bliss.

The grinning spine-walker pattered his footsies up and down her back and shoulders and beautiful buttocks. . . .

When we buckled our seat belts and soared into the mysterious east, Mrs. Rosten-san sighed, "Best massage I ever had in all my life."

I glowered in shameless jealousy.

□   □

A WALK
ON THE BEACH

The sea sings along the sun-drenched beach, not
many minutes from New York, and the waves lick
at my toes like warm puppies' tongues. "Beyond
my heart I need not reach when all is summer
here."

Overhead, the startling gulls blaze white against
the powder-blue sky—hanging, floating, gliders
with a heartbeat; and the ocean that runs from me
to Portugal is paved with diamonds sparkling.

> *Monet taught us how to see light on
> water—or on grass or cathedral stone.
> Did any artist ever try so impossible a
> task as painting the surface of that
> lily pond in his garden? "Endless tor-
> ture," he said, and at eighty-two
> showed Clemenceau the astounding
> Nympheas—a shimmering, 300-foot-
> long miracle I saw in the oval Or-
> angerie in Paris. It is a painting fit
> for paradise.*

The sunburned children are digging their imme-
morial sand castles and moats, clawing out tun-
nels, patting down the towers and ramps with wet
mud—always with the fervent gravity of child-
hood.

> *The Ziggurat had wide ramps, too,
> spiraling up to the shrine on top,
> from which the priests of ancient
> Babylon observed the zodiac. . . .
> Was it Prescott who described the
> great Incan Temple of the Sun, at*

Cuzco, where the sovereigns of Peru
were arrayed in replica, in long rows
—kings on one side, queens on the
other—and the walls "blazed in re-
fulgent gold"?

Muscled bronze men are playing football, scuff-
ing up puffs of sand as they leap and lunge for the
long pass, mimicking the ferocious splendor of
fall's pros.

I once saw "Crazy Legs" Hirsch make
a run for the Los Angeles Rams that
was sheer poetry, and Gale Sayers
break out of tackle in an explosion of
speed and power and grace. . . . And
who of those lucky enough to see it
will ever forget "Red" Grange's four
touchdowns against Pennsylvania?

A bikinied nymph and her Apollo splash out of
the sea, limbs flashing, avoiding the dead fish on
shore, stiff on its side, one cold green eye glaring
at heaven.

Did it, in its last living moment, think
as, I think, we each will: "Why me?
. . . Why now? . . . Why forever?"

Two forlorn girls on shore hug their knees, staring at the meaningless horizon. Grunt: "So tonight?"

Blurt: "Maybe we take in a movie?"

Grunt: "What's playin'?"

Blurt: "I dunno, who *cares,* it's a *movie!"*

So why not? No darkness promises

as much as a movie theater's. No narcotic plunges the self so swiftly into the sweeter other-world of fantasy: other people's dreams and loves and conquests. How many mortals flee their own reveries because they are so impoverished—or so painful, so confused, so inchoate—and replace them with richer phantoms of desire? No wonder Hollywood touched the sticky heart of the world.

The girls who frequent movie palaces,
Know little of psychoanalysis,
In fact, they're annoyed
By Sigmund B. Freud,
And cling to their unconscious phalluses.

Two cocoa-colored towheads take turns with a toy trench spade, digging a hole already deeper than their waists. . . .

If they dig on—down, down, down—will they reach Domdaniel, the submarine cave where Arabian magicians were supposed to dwell?

A mob now. Beyond, the beach is sparsely populated, but here people herd together, eating, drinking, cackling, yammering, frugging to phonographs that blast the eardrums.

Why do they seek such congestion? Do they like the smell of sweat? The

*grating clamor of vulgar voices? Don't
they mind the garbage, the beer
cans, the bottles? On either side of
the mob lies blessed privacy, which
they shun. . . . They must dread
being alone. They must need atavis-
tic reassurance. They need and must
like what they are part of: the herd.*

Beyond this ugly Coney Island, the "nice"
people have staked out their places on the sand,
symbolic islands of withdrawal; a lotioned couple
sprawl, dog snoozing at their feet, and their radio
plays softly. . . .

*Mozart? Piano. Concerto. The one he
wrote upon hearing that his father
was dying. I've played it a hundred
times. No other melody so captures
the nobility of mourning, or speaks
for unshed tears. . . .*

*What's the most beautiful—just
plain beautiful—sound I ever heard?
Yes, oh, yes—the electrifying "so-o-
o-o-ound the trumpet" of the sweet
countertenor in Purcell's* Come, Ye
Sons of Art. *If I ever hear the angels
sing, they'll surely sing like that. . . .*

A shimmering jet draws its chalk line across the
blueboard of the sky, on its way to—Boston,
Athens, Samarkand?

In the west, the clouds have turned pewter, and
crack with far-off lightning. Thunder rolls its

friendly baritone, as summer's thunders do. I turn back.

> The Aztecs thought our world had finished four cycles of the sun: the first when our race was devoured by jaguars, the second when we turned into monkeys, the third in a cataclysm of fire-rain, the fourth when everything drowned in a deluge. Now, we are in the fifth cycle of the sun, which ends—how?

Ahead, the shore wears a veil of mist, crowned by a pink aureole. I glance back: the proud towers of Manhattan, dramatic beyond compare, a luminous lamasery, a city reaching to heaven with an audacity unprecedented in all of history, this gleaming, dazzling palisade of steel and glass—is tipped by the flames of the sun.

I shiver in a premonition of Babylon on fire.

ABOUT THE AUTHOR

Leo Rosten, a writer of remarkable versatility and intellectual range, is the creator of the immortal H*Y*M*A*N K*A*P*L*A*N, Captain Newman, M.D., the phenomenal bestseller *The Joys of Yiddish*, and twenty other books. His name and stories have often appeared on the movie screen. His pioneer studies *Hollywood* and *The Washington Correspondents* are considered classics in social science. "The World of Leo Rosten," in *Look*, was called "the most interesting column being published in America."

A Ph.D. from the University of Chicago, Mr. Rosten studied at the London School of Economics where he is an Honorary Fellow, has taught at Yale, was Ford Visiting Professor at the University of California, and is a Faculty Associate of Columbia University.

His writings have won for him such distinguished citations as the Freedoms Foundation Medal, the George Polk Memorial Award, and the Alumni Professional Achievement Award of the University of Chicago. He is a member of the National Academy of Literature and the Arts.